ⁿ
ir
bur.

2

2

# Irish Social and
# Political Attitudes

# Irish Social and Political Attitudes

*Edited by*
John Garry, Niamh Hardiman and Diane Payne

LIVERPOOL UNIVERSITY PRESS

First published 2006 by
Liverpool University Press
4 Cambridge Street
Liverpool L69 7ZU

British Library Cataloguing-in-Publication data
A British Library CIP record is available


ISBN 0-85323-909-6 cased
ISBN-13 978-0-85323-909-3




Typeset by Northern Phototypesetting Ltd, Bolton
Printed and bound in the European Union by MPG Books Ltd, Bodmin

# Contents

vi    **Contents**

*Appendices*

# List of Tables

# List of Figures

# Contributors

**John Garry**
School of Politics, International Studies and Philosophy, Queen's University Belfast

**Niamh Hardiman**
School of Politics and International Relations, University College Dublin

**Betty Hilliard**
School of Sociology, University College Dublin

**Fiachra Kennedy**
School of Politics and International Relations, University College Dublin

**Mary Kelly**
School of Sociology, University College Dublin

**Michael Marsh**
Department of Political Science, Trinity College Dublin

**Tony McCashin**
Department of Social Studies, Trinity College Dublin

**Brian Motherway**
CPPU, Department of Civil and Environmental Engineering, University College Cork

**Mick O'Connell**
School of Psychology, University College Dublin

**Diane Payne**
School of Sociology, University College Dublin

**Richard Sinnott**
School of Politics and International Relations, University College Dublin

**Nessa Winston**
School of Applied Social Science, University College Dublin

# Introduction

## John Garry and Diane Payne

Ireland has changed radically in the last two decades. The Irish economy has been, by any standards, an amazing success. In stark contrast to the recession, unemployment and emigration of the 1980s and early 1990s, the Irish economy has grown at an unprecedented rate since the mid-1990s, leading to almost full employment and significant increases in average income. Such a rapid achievement of economic prosperity has arguably had a major impact on all walks of Irish life. In tandem with economic growth, there has been growth in the diversity of people living in Ireland. What was a starkly homogeneous society in terms of skin colour and ethnic background is now becoming, slowly but surely, a much more multicultural society. Now that immigration has firmly replaced emigration, serious questions are being raised as to how Irish citizens regard the newcomers: to what extent is there hostility towards the unprecedentedly large numbers of immigrants, refugees and asylum seekers? To what extent are the Irish living up to the stereotype of being friendly, welcoming people?

As well as facilitating a more multicultural society, the major growth in economic activity has profound implications for the environment of Ireland. Now that the key problems of economic depression and unemployment have been dealt with, to what extent do citizens feel the need to prioritize environmental concerns? Should economic growth continue unabated, or should it be regulated and constrained in a context of sustainable development? Recent Irish prosperity has also facilitated a rapid increase in the proportion of women in the workplace. How has this change impacted on people's attitudes to the place of women (and men) in society? Are perceptions of gender roles changing as women increasingly take up positions outside the home? Has the economic prosperity of Ireland brought in its wake a liberalization of attitudes towards the family, work and home life? Furthermore, while it is certainly true that since the appearance of the 'Celtic Tiger', average incomes have risen, *some* people have done a lot better than others. How has the growth in economic inequality that has accompanied rapid economic growth impacted on Irish people's attitudes to relatively impoverished citizens and Irish people's perceptions of the reasons for poverty? In a context of economic opportunity, are Irish citizens more likely to blame poverty on the poor and less likely to view poverty as beyond people's control?

These are some of the key questions this book seeks to answer. To help us find out the answers, we asked Irish people directly. The 2002 Irish Social and Political Attitudes Survey (ISPAS) asked a representative sample of 2,500 people a host of questions about social and political matters.[1] The chapters in this book all draw on Irish people's responses to the Survey questions and offer a wide-ranging and intriguing exploration of contemporary Irish attitudes.

In Chapter 1, Michael O'Connell and Nessa Winston explore attitudes to racial and ethnic minorities. The authors assess the extent to which the increase in ethnic diversity in recent years has led to increased hostility towards minorities. They measure the level of racism in a range of different ways and compare the 2002 results with those from previous surveys in order to assess change in attitudes over time. The authors also explore the extent to which certain social groups, such as young people and the less educated, are particularly likely to be hostile to minorities.

Brian Motherway and Mary Kelly investigate Irish people's attitudes to the environment. In Chapter 2 they report the extent to which people are concerned about environmental matters and assess whether levels of concern have risen or fallen since the early 1990s. The authors explore whether 'green' attitudes are the preserve of certain social groups, such as the young and the well off, or are held in fairly equal measure by all groups. They place their findings in a broad theoretical context by investigating whether Irish attitudes are more in line with the mainstream sustainable development approach to environmental matters than more radical approaches to the environment.

Betty Hilliard assesses the extent to which Irish people may be becoming less traditional in their views on the 'correct' place for women and men in society. In Chapter 3 she explores changes over time in Irish attitudes to gender roles and assesses the extent to which men and women differ in their views on the appropriateness of certain roles.

In Chapter 4, Niamh Hardiman, Tony McCashin and Diane Payne focus on attitudes to poverty and inequality: do Irish people believe that people at the bottom of the economic ladder are there due to their own

---

1. Details of how this survey was conducted are provided in Appendix A. The full questionnaire – with frequency distributions – is provided in Appendix B. The survey was funded by the Programme for Research in Third Level Institutions (PRTL1) of the Higher Education Authority

incompetence and fecklessness, or because of systemic factors beyond their control?

The final three chapters place these discussions of social change in their broader political context and assess how such social developments can be understood in the light of citizens' attitudes to the political system, the nature of competition between the political parties and the fundamental political divisions in contemporary Irish society. In Chapter 5, John Garry explores the extent to which Irish people are alienated from politics. Do people trust institutions such as the Dáil and the legal system? Do they feel that their views are likely to make any difference or that politicians care about their views? How interested are people in politics and how much do they really know about the political world? As well as addressing these questions, Garry investigates whether certain social groups are more alienated than others and what the impact of alienation might be on political behaviour such as turnout and party choice. In Chapter 6, Fiachra Kennedy and Richard Sinnott identify the key underlying political divisions in Ireland. In the context of a comparative European framework, they explore attitudes to the nation state (covering the themes of Northern Ireland, the European Union and Church–State relations) and the economy (egalitarianism and the free market). They identify the demographic correlates of attitudes in each of these areas and the impact of these attitudes on party preferences.

Party preferences is also Michael Marsh's focus in Chapter 7. He explores the extent to which the Irish electorate is 'open to competition' between parties. What proportion of the electorate is firmly in the camp of one particular party (and therefore out of the reach of the other parties, or beyond persuasion)? And what proportion is favourably disposed to a number of parties (and is thus 'open to competition' between them and could potentially vote for any one of them)? Has the proportion of the electorate that is open to party competition – and may be described as 'floating voters' – changed since the late 1980s?

In the Conclusion, the findings of all of the authors are placed firmly in the context of a changing Ireland. Niamh Hardiman elaborates on the key changes in Ireland that stem from the remarkable economic boom of the 1990s. She assesses how the current attitudes of Irish people, as set out in this book, can be understood in the context of an evolving Ireland in an increasingly globalized world.

# 1. Changing Attitudes towards Minorities in Ireland

## *Michael O'Connell and Nessa Winston*

The pattern of declining population growth in Ireland, evident in the middle decades of the last century, has in recent years reversed sharply. In 1991, the census reported a population of 3,526,000. Five years later, this had increased by 100,000. However, in the following six years,[1] the increase in population was almost 300,000. The Central Statistics Office (CSO) figures demonstrate that some of this increase was 'natural', in the sense that it reflects an increase of births over deaths. However, this only accounts for 47 per cent of the increase. The other 53 per cent of the increase was caused by net migration. This 1996–2002 period was one of the few intercensal periods showing positive rather than negative net migration (i.e. showing more people immigrating than emigrating) and is the only intercensal period when the estimated per annum net migration (25,511) exceeds the estimated per annum natural increase (23,030). Ireland – unlike, for example, France – has been historically a country of emigration and the recent phase of immigration has been a novel one.

In 2001, it is estimated that 19,800 people migrated from Ireland, while 46,100 migrated into the country. CSO figures reveal that 43 per cent of immigrants were from the UK or the USA and it seems likely that many of these were Irish nationals returning to live in Ireland because of its strong economic performance at that time. A further 19 per cent were from other EU countries and the remaining 38 per cent, or 17,500, were described as coming from 'rest of world'. What distinguishes this period from the other infrequent ones when net migration was positive (for example, 1971–1979) was the diversity of the migrants. In the past, ethnic, national or religious diversity often came about largely through returning Irish migrants being accompanied by spouses from different backgrounds. However, factors such as improved economic opportunities for immigrants in Ireland and humanitarian crises

---

1. The census planned for April 2001 was postponed until April 2002 because of the threat of an epidemic of foot-and-mouth disease.

and wars in Africa and parts of Eastern Europe have led to a much broader range of people seeking to live in Ireland. In 2001, the Office of the Refugee Applications Commissioner received 10,325 applications for asylum. The top six Countries of Origin (COIs) of the applicants, making up over 61 per cent of the applicants, were Nigeria, Romania, Moldova, Ukraine, Russia and Croatia (First Annual Report of the Office of the Refugee Applications Commissioner, 2002 Appendix 3: 65). Aside from recent asylum seekers who are generally not allowed to work while their claim is being processed, 36,436 temporary (one-year) work/employment visas were also issued to applicants from non-EEA countries[2] in 2001, of which 29,594 were new permits and 6,485 were renewals (source: www.entemp.ie). The countries issued with the highest numbers of these in 2002 were Latvia (3,958), Lithuania (3,816), the Philippines (3,255) and Poland (3,142).[3]

During the period 1996–2000, Ireland was ranked fourth in the EU in terms of the total number of asylum seekers per 1,000 population (*The Economist*, 8 June 2002: 28). Belgium and the Netherlands accept substantially more and Austria marginally more. The report of the Office of the Refugee Applications Commissioner (Appendix 1: 54) comments that Ireland has experienced a 'phenomenal increase in asylum applicants in the past decade from 39 in 1992 to 1,179 in 1996 to 10,938 in 2000'. However, Ireland's increase is described as 'phenomenal' mainly because the starting point was close to zero in the early 1990s. The fact that the numbers of people seeking asylum in Ireland are above the EU average does not mean that their numbers are particularly high. This is because of the increasing lack of sympathy in EU countries for all foreigners, a position parodied in *The Economist* as follows: 'We have vacancies for a limited number of computer programmers and will reluctantly accept torture victims with convincing scars. Migrants looking for a better life can clear off' (13 June 2002). Net migration of 25,511 per annum represents merely 0.006 of the Irish population overall. Very few asylum seekers are offered refugee status in Ireland (467 in 2001) and the population remains relatively homogeneous, especially in comparison with the post-imperial and so-called 'traditional immigration' countries in the EU.

Since the government introduced its policy of dispersal in 1999, asylum seekers are accommodated in reception centres throughout the state where, under the system of direct provision, their basic needs are met while they await a decision on their application for refugee status.

---

2. EEA: The European Economic Area, consisting of the EU states plus Norway, Iceland and Liechtenstein.
3. Given EU enlargement, the citizens of three of these countries are no longer required to apply for work visas.

At present, there are over 70 of these centres in 24 counties, with approximately 5,000 people in direct provision accommodation (Waters, 2002: 12). There are two exceptions to the system of direct provision and dispersal. Some asylum seekers obtain permission on the grounds of illness or family circumstances to move into private rented accommodation. It is estimated that 1,000 such moves were approved in the first 13 months of direct provision (Woods and Humphries, 2001: 8). Thus, the presence of asylum seekers alone in each county in Ireland represents a change in the ethnic make-up of the population around the country. Shops and restaurants catering to new ethnic groups have opened in a number of locations. Media reports and political commentary, not always sympathetic, dealing with new minorities have also appeared. In short, a modest but significant change has occurred in Irish society.

## Response to Change

What has been the public response to this increase in the diversity of the Irish population? One type of reaction might be positive, in that the very fact that there are people seeking asylum or economic opportunities in Ireland may symbolize a certain confidence in the state, especially in comparison with past decades, when at times the viability of the state and its potential to support a population was questioned. However, in Ireland, in particular since 1997, anecdotal reports and comments of those from minority backgrounds appear to indicate that some responses have been negative, crude and indeed at times criminal. An Amnesty International (Ireland) survey found that most black people interviewed, including black Irish citizens, had experienced some kind of abuse, ranging from name-calling to physical abuse (Loyal and Mulcahy, 2001). Those from Asian backgrounds also reported that racism was common. Similarly, another study by Casey and O'Connell (2000) found that the experience of abuse and discrimination was routine for ethnic minorities in Ireland. Irish Government-funded campaigns to combat these acts, such as the kNOw Racism campaign (the National Anti-Racism Awareness Programme, see www.knowracism.ie), approved in 2000 and launched in 2001, also provide indirect evidence of the widespread concerns about the prevalence of hostility towards new minorities. A report in the UK Sunday newspaper *The Observer* on 19 August 2001 paints a very grim picture of 'racist violence and intimidation' in Ireland – a refugee from death squads in the Congo reports the daily experiences of racism he suffers in Ireland: 'I have lived in France and Belgium but I never experienced what I've had here. I've been called nigger and monkey on many occasions.' Tourist guides, presumably with no deliberate agenda to distort the truth, warn visitors of the 'visible and audible racism' prevalent in the capital (*Time Out*, 2002: 23). Experiences ranging from being patronized, to verbal abuse, to perceived discrimination in the workplace and ultimately physical assault (including arson and stabbing) have been reported in the media by people from African, Asian and East European countries living in Ireland and from West Europeans from ethnic minority groups.

It may be the case that most of the Irish population are strongly opposed to racism or, alternatively, it may be that widespread xeno-phobia provides a protective backdrop within which racist acts such as those described above can occur (and the police do not feel obliged to respond actively). What is required in order to assess Irish people's atti-tudes to minorities is a valid survey of the views of a representative sample of the population.[4]

The remainder of this chapter presents the views on minorities of a nationwide sample of Irish adults in 2002. The questions employed in this section, which examine 'Identity and Minorities', are presented in Appendix B at the end of this book. In the analysis below, the aims are threefold:

1. First, we present a description of the views of a representative sample of Irish respondents in contemporary Ireland to questions around the issues of identity and minorities.[5]
2. Second, we examine the direction of change in these views since the mid-1990s. The mid-1990s is selected as an important 'pre-change' comparison point, since (a) the intercensal period 1991–1996 had a net migration rate of only 1,660 compared with 25,511 in the period 1996–2002; (b) the numbers seeking asylum increased from 362 in 1994 to 3,883 in 1997; and (c) many media and anecdotal reports claim that the campaign period prior to the 1997 general election was the first time that racism was felt by many individuals of ethnic

---

4. In an earlier study, based on a Dublin sample, Curry (2000) found high levels of negative attitudes towards minorities, including high levels of social distance from (a dislike of intimacy with) minorities and negative stereotypical views about asylum seekers from various countries.
5. The term 'minorities' is clearly an ambiguous one. Technically for example, adult males in Ireland represent a minority of the adult population. However, the term is used in this chapter in particular to identify those groups of people whose arrival in Ireland especially since the mid-1990s altered the perceived homogeneity of the population. Thus it describes, in short-hand and inevitably loosely, ethnic and national minorities and some religious and pan-geographical ones, which often overlap. For example, one could think of 'Blacks' in Ireland as a recognizable minority, which in turn might include Irish people of colour, people of Afro-Caribbean descent from the UK, French people of African origin, Black Africans (who obvi-ously could then be geographically subdivided), etc. Separately from immigrants, asylum seekers are not necessarily of any ethnic, religious or national origin, but in Ireland have been overwhelmingly Algerian, Congolese, Romanian, Moldovan and Nigerian.

minority origin in the state. Therefore, the questions selected for use in the current survey are for the most part replicated items of those asked either in the Eurobarometer[6] Survey of 1997 or in the ISSP[7] Survey in 1995, both of which focused heavily on attitudes towards immigration, asylum-seeking and national identity. Differences in 'social distance' measures (see below) gathered by MacGreil (1996) in 1988 and in this 2002 survey are also explored.

3.  Third, we identify demographic and attitudinal correlates of social distance and views about minorities. For example: Are those whose views are strongly hostile or negative towards minorities more likely to show a particular profile in terms of education, income, sex or age? Are people's attitudes to race and immigration strongly related to their attitudes to other social and political issues?

## Attitudes to National Identity and to Minorities

Survey respondents were asked to indicate how important they felt that a series of seven attributes were in contributing to a person's 'Irishness' (see Figure 1.1).[8] Two quite different attributes are ranked in the top three – an 'irredentist' factor (being born in Ireland) and a subjective commitment to the country (feeling Irish). Furthermore, the response to the citizenship item is ambiguous, since on the one hand citizenship is technically open to people of all backgrounds under certain circumstances, while it is difficult to obtain for many minority groups. This tension between the perspectives on the meaning and 'achievability' of Irishness was also revealed in the responses to another question in the survey, which asked whether people who did not share Irish customs could become fully Irish: 43.8 per cent agreed/strongly agreed, while 39.2 per cent disagreed/strongly disagreed. Similarly, with regard to support for minorities to receive assistance from the government to preserve their customs, 40.8 per cent agreed while 34.3 per cent disagreed. This captures the disagreement over assimilationist and accommodationist strategies in integrating minorities. In addition, respondents had to decide whether it was better for minority groups to blend into Irish

---

6. A biannual survey of a representative sample of the adult population of each EU member state. This has been ongoing since 1970 and thus provides a unique picture of the evolution of public attitudes on diverse topics across Europe.

7. The International Social Survey Programme (ISSP) consists of biennial assessments of public opinion in various industrialized countries on a number of issues of social importance since 1985.

8. There was also widespread pride among respondents in their Irishness. Of the sample, 97 per cent were either very proud (58.4 per cent) or quite proud (38.6 per cent) to be Irish.

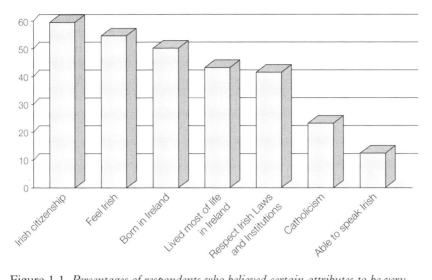

Figure 1.1  *Percentages of respondents who believed certain attributes to be very important aspects of Irishness*

society or to maintain distinct customs. Just under 40 per cent opted for the latter, while over 60 per cent opted for the former view. At this point in the survey, participants were asked to name the groups they considered 'racial and ethnic groups'. Small percentages named specific ethnic, religious or national groups such as Muslims (8.0 per cent), Romanians (6.5 per cent), Travellers (4.0 per cent) and Nigerians (3.0 per cent), but most selected broader categories such as 'all groups' (24.4 per cent), or none in particular (16.4 per cent), or all non-nationals (5.3 per cent), suggesting that people may have a general or broad concept of 'other than white Irish', rather than a series of specific ones.

McConahay (1986) has noted that fascism and Nazism brought overt racism into disrepute. Most people are uncomfortable with accusations of prejudice and wish to be perceived as being at ease with minorities. In this survey, most respondents said they found not at all disturbing the presence of people of another race (64.0 per cent) or another nationality (67.5 per cent), although about one-third did find the presence of other groups at least a little disturbing. Also, between one-fifth and a quarter believed that there were too many people living in Ireland from another nationality (19.9 per cent), another culture (20.3 per cent), or another race (25.2 per cent). And when asked to place themselves on a scale of 1–10, 1 being 'not at all racist' and 10 being 'very racist', 32.9 per cent placed themselves between 4 and 10. These questions therefore reveal that while a majority is explicit in its rejection of the label of racist, about one-third of respondents tend to take up a position ranging from at least a partial acceptance of being prejudiced to outright acknowl-edgement of the label.

The participants were also asked to respond to a number of state-ments about minorities in general. Given the difficulties inherent in defining specifically what was meant by the term 'minority' (see foot-note 5), the respondents were simply asked to react to survey items while 'thinking about different racial and ethnic groups'. Although a large majority had rejected the label of 'racist' and/or did not feel dis-turbed by the presence of minorities, there was a high level of agreement with negative statements about minorities. In Figure 1.2 below, the percentages 'tending to agree' with five negative statements about minorities are presented. These percentages have been recalculated after the 'don't know' responses have been excluded. Almost 70 per cent of those who had a view on the topic stated that they tended to agree that people from different racial and ethnic minority groups abuse the system of social benefits. Approximately 55 per cent of those who expressed a view stated that people from these minority groups increase unemployment in Ireland and that they have an unfair advantage in get-ting local authority housing. Finally, about half of those who offered their views on the topic felt that in schools where there are too many children from these minority groups, the quality of education suffers.

Despite the high levels of agreement with negative statements in Figure 1.2, there was also agreement with a number of positive state-ments. After the 'don't know' responses were excluded, 86.2 per cent

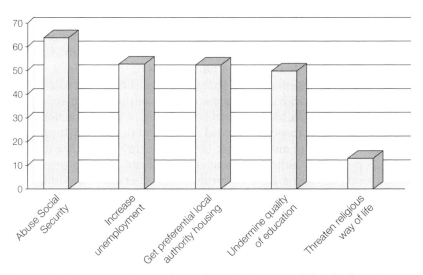

Figure 1.2 *Percentages of respondents who tended to agree (after the don't knows were excluded) with the following negative statements about minorities*

agreed that discrimination in the workplace should be outlawed, 75.4 per cent agreed that the 'authorities should make an attempt to improve things for minorities' and 50 per cent tended to agree that minorities enrich the cultural life of Ireland. Perhaps one interpretation of these varied responses, if one rules out simple acquiescence bias, is that people feel that the rules governing society should be fair, but that some minorities are not adhering to the rules.

A reflection of the wide-scale agreement with negative views of minorities was observable in the high levels of social distance from certain groups that respondents felt. This measure is based on the 'Bogardus' concept of social distance, whereby an individual selects a statement (from seven) that best reflects his or her preferred level of social distance from particular national, ethnic or religious groups (Bogardus, 1933). These range from intimacy (marrying into a family), close friendship, neighbour, co-worker, Irish citizenship, visitors only, to deporting or barring someone from a country.[9] While there is a great deal of variation in the responses, some groups attract very high average scores, suggesting that, overall, the sample preferred to maintain high levels of social distance from the groups in question. The groups most likely to be placed at a greater social distance were Travellers, Muslims, Arabs and Nigerians (see the information relating to 2002 in Figure 1.3 below). There were also relatively high scores for Black Americans, Chinese and Indians (South Asian).

Are people prejudiced against certain groups because they perceive the groups to be wealthy? Using ladders as symbols to represent Irish society, on which the highest rung represented the wealthiest section of Irish society and the lowest rung the least wealthy, participants were asked to indicate where they felt certain groups could be found on average. One reason for the hostility to Travellers may have been the perception held by almost half (44.4 per cent) of the respondents that the Travellers' economic position lay in the wealthier half of society. On the other hand, this view may have been simply a rationalization of prejudice by many. Another important factor in sustaining some of the attitudes may lie in the lack of contact between the indigenous/settled/Irish/white population and people of diverse backgrounds. Participants were asked whether in their neighbourhood, among their workmates or among their friends there were people of different races or cultures.

9. An example of one of the statements used – the midpoint – is as follows; 'Would be willing to work in the same workplace'. Although not without its flaws, the scale has been used many times and allows for comparison across different time periods. Its underlying assumption is that the preference for greater social distance should be reflected in the selection of a statement towards the latter part of the series, which accrues a higher score. The method also permits a comparison to be made in the social distance towards various groups; for example, are people more likely to accept Spaniards as close friends but Nigerians only as workmates?

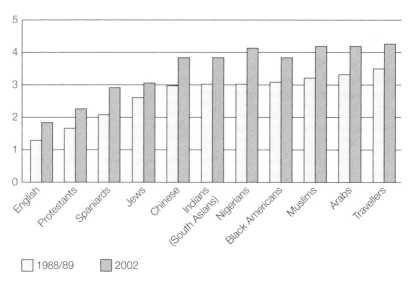

Figure 1.3  *Average social distance to various minority groups (lower scores indicate greater intimacy)*

As Figure 1.4 demonstrates, the proportion of respondents with even some friends or work colleagues from ethnic and cultural minorities is low. In the absence of direct contact, stereotypical views of minorities can easily develop and be sustained (Allport, 1954).

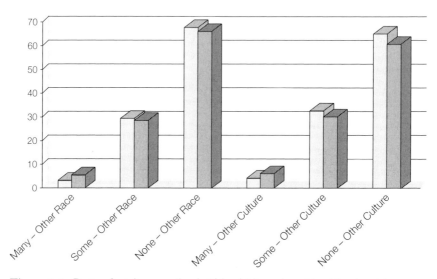

Figure 1.4  *Respondents' contact levels (friendship and work) with minorities*

## Change over Time

Respondents, in both 1997 and 2002, were asked to locate themselves on a ten-point racism scale (with 1 being not at all racist and 10 being very racist). Figure 1.5 reveals the small but significant increases in the proportion of people identifying themselves as racist. Also, in both 1995 and 2002, respondents were asked whether political refugees should be allowed stay in Ireland. The proportion 'strongly agreeing' fell from 22.3 per cent to 14.9 per cent in 2002. It should be noted that under the 1951 Geneva Convention and the related 1967 Protocol, Ireland is *obliged*, as a signatory, to provide asylum for political or other types of refugees where there is a well-founded fear of persecution.

There was also evidence of a growing perception that there were too many 'minorities' now in Ireland. In Figure 1.6, the increasing proportions of those who felt this way in comparison with 1997 is demonstrated. (However, this increase may also be related to the 2002 question asked about 'minorities of a different race' while the 1997 survey asked about 'minorities' in general.)

As noted above, the Bogardus social distance scale facilitates comparisons of how close respondents would like to be to different minority groups. While the least popular groups in the 2002 survey were Travellers, Arabs, Muslims and Nigerians, there has been a particular hardening of attitudes towards Nigerians, since the 1988–89 survey. However, the social distance expressed towards a range of ethnic, racial and religious minorities has increased during the period. (The reader

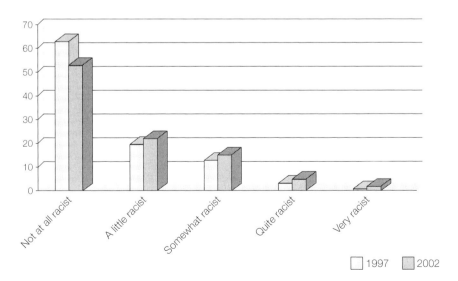

Figure 1.5 *Self-placement of respondents on a racism scale, 1997 and 2002*

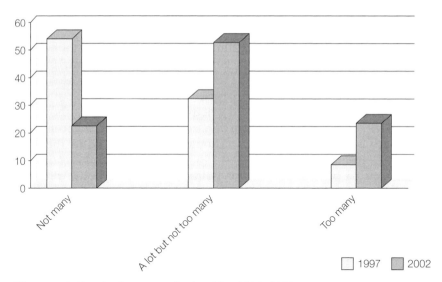

Figure 1.6 *Perceived presence of minorities, 1997–2002*

can visually contrast the responses of the 1988–89 and 2000 by looking back to Figure 1.3.)

Figure 1.7 below contrasts the survey snapshots of 1997 and 2002 on four items, again excluding 'don't knows'. For example, respondents were much more likely to believe that minorities abuse the social welfare system (almost 70 per cent) than they were in 1997 (almost 50 per

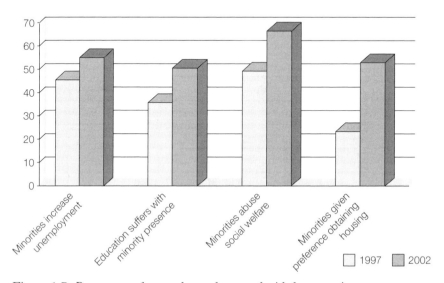

Figure 1.7 *Percentages of respondents who agreed with four negative statements about minorities, 1997–2002*

cent). Similarly, they were significantly more likely to feel that minorities have an unfair advantage in obtaining local authority housing in 2002 (55 per cent) compared with 1997 (25 per cent).

Overall, the presence of minorities in Ireland appears to have coincided with a decline in general sympathy for refugees, a greater social distancing of the population from all minorities and a growing adherence to negative stereotypes about minorities and a belief that they are too prevalent in number.

## Correlates of Prejudice

In this section, we assess the extent to which negative attitudes towards minorities are associated with certain socio-demographic factors. For example, are older people and less-educated people more likely to have negative (or intolerant) attitudes towards minorities than younger or more highly educated people? In order to simplify our analysis, we construct a single measure of 'attitudes to minorities' from the responses to a wide range of the questions discussed in the above sections.[10]

When respondents' positions on this 'attitudes to minorities' scale were compared with social background factors, it emerged that older respondents tended to have more negative attitudes than younger respondents. A stronger relationship emerged in terms of educational qualifications. Education is widely thought to have an impact on civic values generally and tolerance of difference specifically (see Bobo and Licari, 1989). The information here – see Figure 1.8 – confirms this pattern among an Irish sample, with tolerance clearly increasing with level of education.

In addition to socio-demographic correlates, we also examined some attitudinal correlates. Interestingly, the extent to which respondents feel close to Europe is related to their tolerance levels: those who felt closer to Europe had more tolerant attitudes ($p < 0.001$). Pride in Irishness had a stastically significant negative relationship with tolerance ($p = 0.005$) so that respondents who were more proud to be Irish tended to

10. A single 'attitudes towards minorities' measure was created from the following survey questions: degree of disturbance indicated by the presence of people of other races or nationality; degree of un/willingess to allow those suffering political repression elsewhere to find refuge in Ireland; degree to which respondents felt there were too many people of another nationality/race/culture in Ireland; social distance from Nigerians and Travellers (these groups were selected because their social distance measures were highest); self-placement on a 1–10 racism scale; and level of agreement with the following four negative statements: too many children from minority groups undermine education; minorities abuse social welfare; minorities have an unfair advantage in obtaining local authority housing; and minorities threaten our way of life.

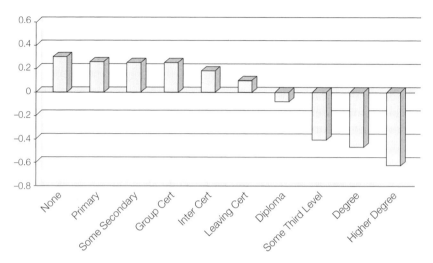

Figure 1.8 *'Minorities' score by educational attainment groups (lower score = greater level of tolerance)*

have more negative attitudes to minorities (although the relationship is not particularly strong). Also, respondents who indicated that in order 'to be truly Irish' one had to be Catholic tended to have strongly intolerant views ($r = -0.29$, $p < 0.001$). The perception of the wealth of Travellers and Romanians (the Cantril 'ladder' questions, see survey questions D11 in Appendix B) were also moderately associated with negative attitudes to minorities: those who perceived these groups (respectively $r=0.25$, $p < 0.001$, and $r = 0.29$, $p < 0.001$) to be better off are more likely to be intolerant.[11]

It also emerged that those who had spent some time living outside Ireland were also likely to have more tolerant attitudes, and that the longer they had lived outside, the greater the impact. This suggests that the experience of more multicultural societies elsewhere was associated with more positive views of minorities.[12] This is in line with the classic social psychological 'contact hypothesis' of Allport, whereby greater exposure of different ethnic groups to one another should reduce intergroup hostility. However, caution must be exerted in interpreting these findings. Respondents were also asked about their contact with people from different races and cultures. There was no significant reduction in the 'attitude to minorities' score where people worked or lived in neigh-

11. The relationship between self-esteem (a combined score) and 'Minorities' was weak and statistically non-significant.
12. Most Irish people emigrate to the UK, the USA or Australia.

bourhoods with more minorities in Ireland. Where people had some or many friends among minority groups, a significant reduction in intolerance was visible, but the causal direction of effect is difficult to discern here. Knowledge of politics generally was associated with greater tolerance. For example, the 35 per cent who recognized that David Byrne was the current Irish commissioner to Europe had a significantly lower score than the majority who did not (sig. $t < 0.001$).[13]

## Conclusion

A modest but significant change has occurred in the ethnic make-up of Irish society, with increases in the number and range of ethnic minorities living there since 1991. Recent studies suggest that these groups experience varying degrees of racism and abuse, ranging from name-calling to physical violence (Loyal and Mulcahy, 2001; Casey and O'Connell, 2000). This raises questions about the extent of racism among Irish nationals and the extent to which their perceptions of minorities living in Ireland are negative or positive.

While most respondents said that they were not at all disturbed by the presence of people of another race (64.0 per cent) or nationality (67.5 per cent), about one-third did find the presence of other groups at least a little disturbing. Moreover, about a quarter felt that there were too many people of another race living in Ireland and 20 per cent felt that there were too many people from other nationalities and cultures in the country. A majority of the sample rejected the label of racist. However, about one-third admitted to either a partial acceptance of being prejudiced or outright acknowledgement of the label. This represents a small but significant increase in the proportion of people identifying themselves as racist since 1997.

Findings from the Bogardus social distance scale reveal that certain groups were less popular with respondents than others. The least popular groups in 2002 were Travellers, Arabs, Muslims and Nigerians. However, the social distance expressed towards a range of ethnic, racial and religious minorities has increased since 1988–89. Another worrying finding is that since 1995 there has been a decline in sympathy for political refugees.

Views of different ethnic minorities, positive and negative, can relate to perceptions that people may have of their cultural traditions and practices. Half of the sample felt that minorities enrich the cultural life

---

13. In a multivariate analysis (not reported here) it emerged that education, having friends from minority groups and having lived outside Ireland were all positively – and statistically significantly – associated with support for minorities.

of Ireland. However, a smaller proportion supported the suggestion that minorities should receive assistance from the government to preserve their customs. Moreover, a clear majority of the respondents felt that it was better for minority groups to blend into Irish society rather than maintain their distinct customs. The sample was divided on the issue of whether people who did not share Irish customs could ever become fully Irish.

The survey revealed a high level of agreement with negative statements about minorities. Large proportions stated that people from different racial and ethnic minority groups abuse the system of social benefits, increase unemployment in Ireland and have an unfair advantage in getting local authority housing. Furthermore, compared with 1997, there were substantial increases in the proportions agreeing with these negative statements.

On a more positive note, almost 90 per cent agreed that discrimination should be outlawed and three-quarters agreed that the authorities should make an attempt to improve things for minorities in Ireland. One possible explanation that we noted for this is that people may feel that rules should be fair, but that some members of the minorities are not adhering to the rules. These findings suggest that there is a need to transmit more information about minorities in Irish society, particularly in relation to their entitlements, economic status and qualifications. The finding that the proportion of respondents with even some friends or work colleagues from ethnic and cultural minorities is low also supports the need for more information. The absence of direct contact with minorities appears to facilitate and sustain stereotypical negative views of minorities. Informing people about minorities and promoting contact with them would be likely to challenge these views and assist in the integration of minorities into Irish society. Additional support for this approach lies in the finding that, controlling for other factors, education, having friends from minority groups and having lived outside Ireland are all positively associated with support for minorities.

## References

Allport, G. W. (1954), *The Nature of Prejudice*. Boston, MA: Addison-Wesley.

Bobo, L., and F. C. Licari (1989), 'Education and Political Tolerance', *Public Opinion Quarterly* 53: 285–308.

Bogardus, E. S. (1933), 'A Social Distance Scale', *Sociology and Social Research* 17: 265–71.

Casey, S., and M. O'Connell (2000), 'Pain and Prejudice: Assessing the Experience of Racism in Ireland', in M. MacLachlan and M. O'Connell (eds.), *Cultivating Pluralism: Psychological, Social and Cultural Perspectives on a Changing Ireland.* Dublin: Oak Tree Press.

Curry, P. (2000), '"She never let them in...": Popular Reactions to Refugees arriving in Dublin', in M. MacLachlan and M. O'Connell (eds.), *Cultivating Pluralism: Psychological, Social and Cultural Perspectives on a Changing Ireland.* Dublin: Oak Tree Press.

Loyal, S., and A. Mulcahy (2001), 'Racism in Ireland: The Views of Black and Ethnic Minorities' (report published in conjunction with FAQs research). Dublin: Amnesty International.

MacGréil, M. (1996), 'Prejudice in Ireland Revisited. Dublin'. Survey and Research Unit, Maynooth.

McConahay, J. B. (1986), 'Modern Racism, Ambivalence, and the Modern Racism Scale', in J. Dovidio and S. Gaertner (eds.), *Prejudice, Discrimination, and Racism.* New York: Academic Press.

Office of the Refugee Applications Commissioner (2002), 'Annual Report 2001'. Dublin: Office of the Refugee Applications Commissioner.

*Time Out Guide to Dublin* (2002), London: Penguin.

Waters, Noel (2002), 'Emerging Challenges in Housing Refugees'. Paper presented at the Clann Housing Association Conference, 'Housing and Refugees: A New Challenge'. Dublin, May 1 2002.

Woods, M., and N. Humphries (2001), 'Statistical Update: Seeking Asylum in Ireland'. Dublin. Social Science Research Centre.

# 2. Evolving Environmental Concern in Ireland: Is Sustainable Development Taking Root?

*Brian Motherway and Mary Kelly*[1]

Some environmentalists regard economic growth and care for nature as incompatible. Others – such as advocates of sustainable development – believe that it is possible for economic development and environmental protection to go hand in hand, as long as economic decision-makers take great care to ensure that the impact of growth on the natural world is minimized. According to the 1987 UN report 'Our Common Future', sustainable development is 'development that meets the needs of the present without compromising the ability of future generations to meet their own needs'. Thus, the sustainable development approach emphasizes the need to avoid short-term thinking about economic matters. Current growth should be encouraged in such a way that it does not use up or destroy the Earth's resources, thus facilitating the maintenance of economic growth over the long term. Advocates of sustainable development typically have faith in science and expertise, and in the possibility of technical solutions to environmental problems. They also have little commitment to radical social or economic reform, based on the belief that the current system can be fairly readily adapted to the imperatives of environmental management.

The sustainable development approach is often perceived (by its subscribers) as a more rational, modern, intelligent version of environmentalism than a *romantic* model of caring for nature, the latter being seen as emotional and lacking a coherent basis. The sustainable development outlook also contrasts with radical movements such as the

1. This analysis is part of the Research Programme on Environmental Attitudes, Values and Behaviour in Ireland, carried out by the Department of Sociology of University College Dublin; the Department of Sociology, Trinity College, Dublin; and the Social Science Research Centre, UCD. Funded through the Environmental Research Technological Development and Innovation Programme, under the Productive Sector Operational Programme 2000-2006. Grant no. 2001-MS/5E1-M1. The programme is financed by the Irish Government under the National Development Plan. It is administered on behalf of the Department of the Environment and Local Government by the Environmental Protection Agency which has the statutory function of co-ordinating and promoting environmental research.

anti-globalization movement, whose agenda is much wider than 'tweaking' the current system to be more environmentally friendly.

The sustainable development approach has grown very significantly in influence since its emergence in the 1970s and its dominance as an environmental discourse was illustrated at the World Summit on Sustainable Development in Rio de Janeiro in 1992. In Ireland, the discourse is obvious in pivotal policy statements such as 'Sustainable Development, A Strategy for Ireland' (Department of Environment, 1997) and also in many developing policy areas such as local government reform (Interdepartmental Taskforce, 2000), climate change abatement (Department of Environment and Local Government, 2000; Department of Public Enterprise, 1999) and planning (Brady Shipman Martin, 1999). The environment has increasingly been put at the centre of policy-making and planning in Ireland, and the notion of sustainable development has been integrated into decision-making in a way that previous environmental discourses never were.[2]

The key aim of this chapter is to examine whether the establishment of sustainable development as a political discourse in Ireland is matched by its growth as a discourse of environmental concern among the general public. By its nature, sustainable development should represent a broader church than more radical environmental discourses. Most notably, sustainable development allows a proponent of the economic growth paradigm to subscribe also to pro-environment politics, whereas most previous versions of environmentalism positioned these in opposition. Thus, the language of sustainability should facilitate a broadening of support for environmentalism. In other words, if there has indeed been a shift towards sustainable development as a discourse of concern among the public, environmentalism should have become more *main*stream than *ex*treme and concern for the environment should no longer be the preserve of distinct social groups but should instead be fairly evenly distributed across the population as a whole.

Thus, our test of growing support for sustainable development may be seen as threefold. Is there a growth in generalized environmental concern across the population and a decline in 'extreme' views about the environment? Is there a pattern of spreading support across socio-demographic categories? Is there increased support for statements specifically encapsulating elements of the sustainable development paradigm, such as the compatibility of economic growth and environmental protection?

2. The incorporation of the sustainable development discourse into mainstream policy discourses is often termed 'ecological modernization'. See, for example, Hajer (1995, 1996).

## Comparing Environmental Concern over Time

We assess the level of Irish people's concern about environmental threats and the extent to which such levels of concern may have changed over time. We draw on responses to a series of questions – included in the ISPAS 2002 Survey and a preceding ISSP 1993 Survey – that asked respondents how dangerous they thought specific pollution sources were to the environment (see Table 2.1).[3]

Table 2.1 *Concern about specific environmental threats*

| | Extreme concern (%) | | Any concern (%) | |
|---|---|---|---|---|
| *How dangerous do you think that . . .* | *2002* | *1993* | *2002* | *1993* |
| Air pollution caused by cars is to the environment? | 14 | 16 | 89 | 84 |
| Air pollution caused by cars is to you and your family? | 6 | 14 | 75 | 76 |
| Air pollution caused by industry is to the environment? | 18 | 26 | 92 | 93 |
| Pesticides and chemicals used in farming are to the environment? | 15 | 24 | 90 | 90 |
| Pollution of Ireland's rivers, lakes and streams is to the environment? | 22 | 36 | 93 | 95 |
| A rise in the world's temperature caused by the "greenhouse effect" (global warming) is to the environment? | 18 | 25 | 86 | 84 |
| In general, nuclear power stations are* | 45 | 53 | 95 | 96 |
| N | 1253 | 957 | 1253 | 957 |

* For this question 'Extreme concern' includes those respondents who answered 'extremely dangerous'. 'Any concern' includes those who answered 'extremely', 'very', or 'somewhat' dangerous.

All questions elicited less extreme concern in 2002 than in 1993. However, the 'any concern' levels (which include not only responses stating that this environmental issue was considered extremely danger-ous but also those responses that stated that they were considered very or somewhat dangerous) did not reduce by nearly as much, and in some

3. In 1993, each item was asked twice, once regarding how dangerous it is to the environment and once regarding how dangerous it is 'to you and your family'. Results suggested that people did not find this distinction meaningful, so in the 2002 survey most of the items were asked just once, in relation to danger to the environment. A smaller number of pollution sources were presented in the 2002 questionnaire, and this analysis is based on the seven items common to both surveys.

cases they increased. Nuclear power stations remained by far the highest concern, both in terms of extreme and 'any concern', followed by pollution of rivers and lakes. The perceived danger posed by air pollution from cars 'for the environment' showed the largest increase in any concern and the least decrease in extreme concern, indicating the elevation of this issue among people's priorities.

Table 2.2 reports the number of items in relation to which respondents expressed extreme concern or 'any concern' (extreme, very or somewhat). It is notable that, despite the large drop in extreme concern responses, for most items there is very little change in the numbers of people who expressed some level of concern. Thus, we find partial support for our first test. There appears a definite decline in 'extreme' views on the environment but not an obvious increase in generalized concern.

Table 2.2 *Extent of expressed concern*

| Number of items | Extreme concern (%) | | Any concern (%) | |
| --- | --- | --- | --- | --- |
| | *2002* | *1993* | *2002* | *1993* |
| 0 | 40 | 30 | 1 | 1 |
| 1 | 28 | 22 | 1 | 0 |
| 2 | 12 | 15 | 2 | 1 |
| 3 | 7 | 14 | 2 | 3 |
| 4 | 5 | 7 | 4 | 5 |
| 5 | 4 | 6 | 9 | 11 |
| 6 | 2 | 4 | 20 | 17 |
| 7 | 2 | 3 | 62 | 61 |
| N | 1253 | 957 | 1253 | 957 |

## Structural Patterns in Environmental Concern

If there is indeed a shift towards the more moderate – sustainable development – paradigm of concern, which is less challenging to dominant institutions and values than other radical environmental paradigms, it should be possible to see subscription to the paradigm from a wider range of constituencies than would be seen for the more radical discourse. This is in keeping with the broader concept of the 'new environmental paradigm' (Dunlap and Van Liere, 1978). Accordingly, the traditional view of environmentalism as the preserve of middle-class, educated urbanites (see, for example, Yearley, 1995), should become less and less true as environmental concern becomes more pervasive (Dietz et al., 1998).

Table 2.3 correlates the number of items on which a respondent expressed extreme concern or any level of concern by socio-demographic variables. As can be seen, 'any concern' levels exhibit greater correlations with the socio-demographic variables than do extreme concern levels.

Table 2.3 *Concern levels correlated with socio-demographic variables*

|  |  | *Correlation with extreme concern level* | *Correlation with any concern level* | *N* |
|---|---|---|---|---|
| Gender of respondent | *2002* | .06 | .05 | 1253 |
|  | *1993* | .04 | .03 | 957 |
| Age of respondent | *2002* | −.01 | −.08* | 1229 |
|  | *1993* | −.13* | −.18* | 953 |
| Highest level of education completed | *2002* | .00 | .14* | 1251 |
|  | *1993* | .17* | .16* | 955 |
| Income level | *2002* | −.01 | .16* | 1044 |
|  | *1993* | .04 | −.01 | 822 |

In both 2002 and 1993, gender showed little effect relative to either any or extreme concern. Expressions of concern (both extreme and any) were less dependent on age in 2002 than they were in 1993. The same pattern is seen for level of education. By contrast, the level of any concern showed a stronger relationship with income in 2002 than in 1993 (i.e. higher income predicts more concern). Significant correlations are seen in 2002, when the total number of items expressed as any level of concern was higher among lower age groups, and people with higher levels of education and higher incomes.

The extent of extreme concern expressed was less related to socio-demographic variables in 2002 than it was in 1993. However, the extent of any concern, the key factor for the more moderate environmentalism of sustainable development, showed mixed results. For age and education, the relationships were weaker in 2002, but the relationship to income had become stronger. Thus, the social bases of environmental concern seem just as strong in 2002 as they were in 1993, although wealth replaced youth as the key predictor of environmental concern.

## Types of Environmental Concerns

The key step in further examining the evidence for a trend towards sustainable development thinking is to look at survey items that ask specifically about elements of the paradigm itself.

The characteristics of the sustainable development paradigm include the placement of environmental protection imperatives as a significant political priority, but in a framework of faith in science and technical solutions, and the belief that environmental and economic growth objectives can be successfully married. These elements can be tested in the survey data through responses to relevant attitudinal questions. In particular, a group of questions was fielded in both 1993 and 2002 that enquired about attitudes to the environment in relation to science and economics, and these can be examined to illuminate any trends in relation to the sustainable development position on these issues.

Table 2.4 *Attitudes towards science*

|  | Net level of agreement | | Neutral responses | |
|  | 2002 | 1993 | 2002 | 1993 |
| --- | --- | --- | --- | --- |
| We believe too often in science, and not enough in feelings and faith | 29 | 43 | 26 | 15 |
| Overall, modern science does more harm than good | −37 | −9 | 22 | 16 |
| Modern science will solve our environmental problems with little change to our way of life | −28 | −31 | 30 | 19 |
| N | 1253 | 957 | 1253 | 957 |

**Note:** Net level of agreement is calculated as a percentage of the respondents who answered 'strongly agree' or 'agree', minus the percentage who answered 'strongly disagree' or 'disagree'. Neutral responses are calculated as a percentage of those who answered 'neither agree or disagree', plus a percentage of those who answered 'can't choose'.

Table 2.4 presents levels of net agreement with each statement – the percentage of those who agreed minus the percentage of those who disagreed. Thus a positive net agreement indicates more agreement than disagreement with the statement, while a negative net agreement indicates more disagreement than agreement.

Responses to the first two items above clearly indicate a greater level of comfort with the role of science in decision making in 2002 than in 1993. Interestingly, though, this does not equate to agreement that science will be able to 'solve our environmental problems with little change to our way of life'. This statement is somewhat double-barrelled, and people may have been addressing the element relating to change in our way of life rather than the role of science. There is evidence to suggest that the first two items were taken as more abstract, philosophical questions, while the third was taken as the more practical issue of optimism about environmental protection being possible 'with little change to our way of life'.

This apparent paradox would suggest that, as postulated by Beck (1992), people have an ambivalent relationship with science and modernity; science is seen as the cause of environmental problems and, at the same time, an important source of solutions to these problems. The pattern in 2002 seems to be greater recognition of the inevitability of environmental damage in modernity, and, at the same time, an increased faith in the same modernity to offer solutions.

Table 2.4, then, suggests that there is indeed growing support for the place of science in decision-making, which would fit with the sustainable development view.

Table 2.5: *Attitudes towards the environment and economic growth*

|  | Net level of agreement | |
|  | 2002 | 1993 |
| --- | --- | --- |
| We worry too much about the future of the environment and not enough about prices and jobs today | −28 | −17 |
| Almost everything we do in modern life harms the environment | 19 | 9 |
| People worry too much about human progress harming the environment | −19 | −7 |
| In order to protect the environment Ireland needs economic growth | 20 | 43 |
| Economic growth always harms the environment | −30 | −19 |
| N | 1253 | 957 |

What about the relative prioritization of economic growth and environmental protection? Several questions in the survey addressed this issue (see Table 2.5). The trend towards prioritization of environmental protection over economic growth is clear in the above responses. The first three items clearly signal a growth in concern about the environment and environmental destruction. The first item shows the most striking move away from the tendency to de-prioritize environmental protection in the face of concerns about employment and economic well-being. The dramatic changes in the economic contexts in which the two surveys were fielded are undoubtedly a major factor here, and their influence is very apparent.[4]

These three questions embody the classic dichotomy often posited between environmental protection and economic growth. However, while allowing respondents to declare their relative priorities, they do not allow them to accept or reject the idea of a dichotomy between economic growth and protecting the environment. The last two items in Table 2.5 address this issue. The last item, in particular, asks whether growth and environmental protection are inevitably in opposition, and the results show that fewer people thought this was so in 2002 than in 1993. At the same time, fewer respondents thought that growth is necessary to protect the environment, possibly reflecting the lower imperative for growth at the end of a decade of boom.

So there is evidence of a shift away from prioritization of economic growth over environmental protection. Moreover, there is evidence that this is more to do with a growing perception of alignment of the goals rather than a simple shift in alternative prioritizations. This possible alignment supports the notion of a move towards the sustainable development paradigm. While the trend away from seeing economic growth and environmental protection as opposing imperatives may indeed indicate uptake of the sustainable development version of environmental concern, it is not out of the question that the underlying trend is simply a lowering in environmental prioritization, showing up as a lesser degree of concern about relative priorities. In other words, respondents who said that they saw growth and environmental protection as aligned may have done so because they saw environmental protection as a weak concern, insufficient to merit a deviation from the growth model. In order to test for this, it is necessary to consider the above responses together with the responses about specific environmental concern discussed earlier in this chapter. Subscribers to the sustainable development paradigm are not sceptical about environmental problems; they are concerned about these risks and wish to see them addressed.

As discussed earlier, responses to questions about specific environmental problems indicate that the level of any concern was much the same in 2002 as in 1993, but responses tended to be less extreme. How do these expressions of concern relate to some of the economy and science questions?

This can be examined by calculating the mean number of items each respondent expresses concern about from the set of seven that were discussed earlier (see Tables 2.1. and 2.2) and then calculating these means

4. The late 1990s were a period of exceptional economic growth in Ireland, commonly referred to as the 'Celtic Tiger' years, with GDP growth far above EU and OECD averages, and unemployment falling to its lowest levels in the history of the State (see Hardiman et al., Chapter 4).

for the subsets of people who agree or disagree with some of the key questions about science or economic growth. Responses in 2002 to two statements – 'Overall, modern science does more harm than good' and 'Economic growth always harms the environment' – are tested in Table 2.6.

Table 2.6 *Extent of concern for the environment, broken down by attitudes to science and the economy, 2002*

|  | *Mean number of extreme concern items* | *Mean number of any concern items* | *N* |
|---|---|---|---|
| Mean among all respondents | 1.4 | 6.2 | 1253 |
| Mean among those who agree or strongly agree that: | | | |
| Overall, modern science does more harm than good | 1.8 | 6.3 | 257 |
| Economic growth always harms the environment | 1.7 | 6.4 | 264 |
| Mean among those who disagree or strongly disagree that: | | | |
| Overall, modern science does more harm than good | 1.4 | 6.4 | 719 |
| Economic growth always harms the environment | 1.3 | 6.3 | 638 |

Table 2.6 gives some insight into the relative extent of concern expressed among those who answered these specific attitudinal questions differently. Those who agreed with the two statements, i.e. who believe that science does more harm than good and that economic growth always harms the environment, tended to express higher levels of extreme environmental concern – the mean environmental concern scores were 1.8 and 1.7 among those who agreed with the statements, as opposed to the overall mean score of 1.4. This is to be expected, as this subset of respondents should include those who tend towards more radical environmental views.

On the other hand, those who disagreed with these statements did not show an appreciable decrease in extreme concern. This indicates that those who express support for the place of science or for economic growth do not necessarily do so on the basis of lack of environmental concern. Patterns are more difficult to discern among the 'any concern' respondents.

This analysis addresses the possible suggestion that some patterns of response on specific attitudinal questions that appear to indicate a move towards sustainable development thinking may simply be reflecting a decrease in environmental concern. It seems, however, that this is not that case, and that the attitudinal questions do indeed provide evidence for a growth in support for the specific type of environmental concern encapsulated in the sustainable development discourse.

## Conclusions

The ISPAS environment module offers valuable insights into the environmental attitudes and behaviours of Irish people in 2002. In addition, the availability of a dataset based on broadly the same questionnaire from 1993 allows for comparison across a turbulent decade in social, economic and environmental terms.

Environmental concern remained in many ways as high in 2002 as it was in 1993, showing the longevity – and presumably the long-term institutionalization and incorporation by the general population – of environmental politics and general prioritization of environmental protection. However, the maintenance of a high level of concern was only true for concern in general and not for levels of extreme concern expressed. While levels of 'any concern' remained steady, extreme concern dropped considerably.

The hypothesis of this chapter is that this pattern does not indicate a decline in environmental concern per se, but rather a mainstreaming of this concern across the population and into normal political discourses. The emblem of this mainstreaming is taken to be the development of the discourse of sustainable development. This paradigm is a discourse of environmentalism that seeks to align economic development and environmental protection by prioritizing environmental efficiency as a means to protecting growth, enhancing economic efficiency, and amending the modern economic and social institutions to accommodate environmentalism in a way that ensures their continuation. While it is clear that this way of thinking has taken firm hold in political discourses, the central question of this chapter has been whether this has translated into a new pattern of environmental concern among people at large.

It has been argued that evidence for this shifting concern pattern would come from a growth in levels of 'any environmental concern', particularly moderate concern; from a spreading of this concern across socio-demographic categories and out of the traditional domains of environmentalism; and from trends towards sustainable development-oriented responses to specific attitudinal questions relating to elements of the paradigm.

By 1993, the environment as a personal and political issue was already well established, and the survey measured high levels of environmental concern among respondents. Levels of concern seen in the 2002 data are similarly high, but do not suggest any significant growth in concern levels as measured through questions about specific environmental threats. Thus the first test, that levels of any concern should be seen to rise, is not passed, unless one hypothesis that a decline in radical views shifts directly to growth in more moderate views.

However, the second part of the test on levels of any concern is that there should be a shift towards moderate versions of concern, and this is certainly a pattern seen in the datasets. No doubt, stronger evidence for growing subscription to the sustainable development paradigm would come from a move from no concern to moderate concern. However, the pattern that is observed here – a move from extreme to moderate concern – does still support the idea that more radical forms of environmentalism are indeed being replaced by the more mainstream version of concern encapsulated in sustainable development. Concern could be less extreme because the issue has become an everyday part of political and general discourse.

This view is further supported to a degree by the socio-demographic patterns among these responses. There is some evidence of a flattening out of the socio-demographic profile of those expressing environmental concern, but the evidence is inconclusive. Moderate concern ('any concern' responses) exhibits greater socio-demographic spread than extreme concern, and lower age, higher education and higher income all predict greater concern. Age and education level, however, decreased in influence between 1993 and 2002. Interestingly, gender demonstrates little influence.

Possibly most insight into the hypothesized trend towards sustainable development versions of concern comes from a number of attitudinal questions which, although not designed to test the sustainable development concept, touch on key elements of the paradigm and thus allow for its examination. These questions relate to attitudes about science, economic growth, and their interaction with environmental issues.

As mentioned, expressed environmental concern was at a high level in 1993. However, in the economic context of the time, a considerable degree of opposition was seen between environmental protection and economic growth goals. By 2002, perceptions of this dichotomy had certainly diminished, and it was possible for respondents to express concern about the environment and yet not see the need to make a choice between environmental and economic imperatives.

This pattern seems to support the hypothesis of a shift towards sustainable development thinking. Respondents who subscribe to this way of thinking would tend to express environmental concern, but not see prioritization of environmental protection as incompatible with an economic growth paradigm. They would also express faith in the role of science in decision-making and in the possibility of technical solutions to many environmental problems. A trend towards these kinds of response sets can be seen when the data for 1993 and 2002 are compared.

Thus, overall there is evidence to support the hypothesis that sustainable development is being translated from a political discourse into a mode of general, popular environmental concern. However, the evidence from the ISPAS environment module is not entirely conclusive. Other research on popular environmental attitudes and discourses currently under way in the wider Research Programme on Environmental Attitudes, Values and Behaviour, of which the analysis presented above is but a part, should illuminate these issues further.

As the political profile and urgency of environmental issues grow, an understanding of the attitudes and views of the general public towards the issues becomes more important than ever. It is clear that overly simplified ideas of one homogeneous concept of the environment, or concern for it, are inadequate. People's perceptions of their surroundings, of nature and of the meaning of environmental threats cannot be reduced to single linear scales of environmental interest or concern.

Now that sustainable development is strongly established in political and institutional terms, it is a question of considerable importance as to whether it encapsulates a model of concern and proposed response to which many people subscribe. Insofar as it has, to date, tended to translate into an expert-oriented discourse, it may run the risk of excessive dependence on scientific or technocratic understandings of the issues in a way that excludes people outside the technical or policy-making circles. It is clear that if people are not allowed to express their own meanings of their environment and its protection, no meaningful progress will be made towards any version of an environmentally sustainable society.

# References

Beck, U. (1992), *Risk Society*. London: Sage.

Brady Shipman Martin (1999), 'Strategic Planning Guidelines for the Greater Dublin Area'. Dublin: Brady Shipman Martin Consultants.

Department of Environment (1997), 'Sustainable Development: A Strategy for Ireland'. Dublin: Stationery Office.

Department of Environment and Local Government (2000), 'National Climate Change Strategy'. Dublin: Department of Environment and Local Government.

Department of Public Enterprise (1999), 'Green Paper on Sustainable Energy'. Dublin: Department of Public Enterprise.

Dietz, T., P. C. Stem and G. A. Guagnano (1998), 'Social Structural and Social Psychological Bases of Environmental Concern', *Environment and Behaviour* 30: 450–71

Dunlap, R., and K. Van Liere. (1978). 'The New Environmental Paradigm: A Proposed Measuring Instrument and Preliminary Results', *Journal of Environmental Education* 9.

Hajer, M. (1995), *The Politics of Environmental Discourse*. Oxford: Oxford University Press.

Hajer, M. (1996), 'Ecological Modernization as Cultural Politics', in Scott Lash et al. (eds.), *Risk, Environment and Modernity: Towards a New Ecology*. London: Sage.

Interdepartmental Taskforce on the Integration of Local Government and Local Development Systems (2000), 'A Shared Vision for County/City Development Boards: Guidelines on the CDB Strategies for Economic, Social and Cultural Development'. Dublin: Department of Environment and Local Government.

Yearley, S. (1995), 'The Social Shaping of the Environmental Movement', in P. Clancy, S. Drudy, K. Lynch and L. O'Dowd (eds.), *Irish Society – Sociological Perspectives*. Dublin: Institute of Public Administration: 652–74.

# 3. Changing Gender Roles in Intimate Relationships

## *Betty Hilliard*

The Irish family has changed considerably over the last quarter of a century (Fahey and Russell, 2001). Demographic factors such as the growth in long-term cohabitation, an explosion in non-marital births, later age at marriage, smaller family size and an increase in the number of mothers entering or remaining in the paid workforce have all contributed to this change. Attitudes towards the family have also changed, away from the familism that Arensberg and Kimball (2001) saw as characterizing traditional Irish rural life, and towards an individualism widely associated with modernity. Related to demographic and value change is change in what are perceived as appropriate gender roles for males and females in long-term relationships. It is with this issue of changing gender roles that this chapter is concerned.

Until recently, when examining the gender roles of partners in long-term relationships, it seemed unproblematic to speak of these as spousal or family roles. The image of 'family' that dominated the social sciences (and, indeed, the media) in the Western world for over half a century owed much to the hegemonic position of Talcott Parsons in English-language sociology, and particularly in the sociology of the family (see Morgan, 1975: 25). The model of the 'normal' family he promulgated was of a union of husband and wife in which roles were divided on the basis of sex. Influenced by the functionalist ideas of writers such as Bales and Slater (1956), he portrayed female roles as primarily affective or expressive and male roles as almost exclusively instrumental or task-oriented (Parsons, 1956).

This limited vision of normal family structure and of male and female roles in long-term relationships was challenged in the 1960s and 1970s by historical scholarship and by the theoretical and empirical advances of feminist research. The work of Peter Laslett and other historians and demographers of the Cambridge School questioned the idea of a 'typical' family form in Europe (Anderson, 1980). Feminists such as Jesse Bernard (1973), Anne Oakley (1974) and Diana Leonard Barker and Sheila Allen (1976) challenged the gender stereotyping of roles and exposed the many dimensions of male and female roles in marriage. In Ireland, Fahey (1992) and O'Hara (1994) drew attention to the essentially economic character of much of the 'female' role in families, as Oakley (1976) and Delphy and Leonard (1992) had done in different ways. Contemporary demographics alerted us to the variation in forms of family formation within and across cultures even in modern Western society. In Ireland, in the 1996 census, the total number of private households was 1,115,000, of which 72.4 per cent were family units. The family form of husband and wife with children constituted just three out of five of these family units; the substantial remainder of family units included lone-parent families, married couples without children and cohabiting couples with and without children.

Thus, for scholars of family life the old certainties are a luxury no longer to be enjoyed. Indeed, it is argued that we cannot now speak of *the* family in any meaningful way, given the diversity of family forms identified both between and within cultures (Bernardes, 1985; Boh, 1989). It is for this reason that the term 'intimate relationships' is used in this chapter; it embraces non-married cohabiting heterosexual couples, as well as reconstituted families and the more traditional forms of family.

Using data from the 2002 Irish Social and Political Attitudes Survey (ISPAS) and previous comparable surveys conducted in 1994 and 1998 (as part of the ISSP survey programme), this chapter reports Irish citizens' attitudes to gender roles, work and family, and domestic tasks.

## Attitudes to Gender Roles, Marriage and Parenthood

Many commentators believe that since the 1960s, gender roles have undergone significant change. Young and Willmott argued in 1973 that gender roles in the family had become *symmetrical*, claiming that a massive transformation had taken place in the status of women in spousal relationships. This so-called 'equality hypothesis' soon came to be challenged, however, by the empirical and theoretical explorations of Pahl and Pahl (1971), Edgell (1980) and Harris (1983) among others, who argued that the theoretical assumptions and methodological and conceptual bases of this hypothesis were seriously flawed.

My aim here is to explore whether such a massive transformation has indeed occurred in Ireland in terms of citizens' attitudes to gender roles. It is clear that support for the stereotypical view of male breadwinner and female housewife changed significantly over a relatively short period. Forty-one per cent of respondents agreed or strongly agreed in 1988 with the statement that 'a man's job is to earn money; a women's job is to look after home and family'. This had declined to 35 per cent in 1994 and 18 per cent in 2002. It emerges that rejection is strongest among the divorced, young people and those attending religious service less than once a week. Also, there was a clear gender difference in 2002 in that 72 per cent of women disagreed with this statement compared with 62 per cent of men. Social class, as measured by occupation, was also significant in that unskilled manual workers were twice as likely to *agree* with this statement compared with those in the higher managerial or professional category.

In 1988, almost half (47 per cent) of all respondents believed that 'married people are generally happier than non-married people'. This dropped to 33 per cent in 1994 and 31 per cent in 2002. Interestingly, when those who did not express a view are excluded, only 35 per cent of women, compared with 47 per cent of men, agreed that married people are happier than non-married.

Traditional attitudes to cohabitation and divorce underwent considerable change from 1994 to 2002 (see Table 3.1). Tolerance for cohabiting unions is on the increase. In 1994, half of all respondents agreed with the statement that 'it is all right for a couple to live together without being married'. Less than a decade later, in 2002, 60 per cent agreed. In response to a related statement – that it is a good idea for couples to live together first before marrying – the proportions who agreed and disagreed were similar (51 per cent and 61 per cent respectively). Those who were never married, the divorced and those who were separated were highest in their support for cohabitation, but there was no significant difference between the views of men and women. Support for divorce also grew in this period.

Table 3.1 *Statements about cohabitation and divorce asked in 1994 and 2002 (percentage of those who agreed)*

| Statement | 1994 | 2002 |
| --- | --- | --- |
| It is all right for a couple to live together without being married | 51 | 60 |
| It is a good idea for a couple who intend to get married to live together first | 51 | 61 |
| Divorce is usually the best solution when a couple can't seem to work out their marriage problems | 51 | 58 |

In contemporary Ireland, parenting seems to be more highly valued than marriage. In 1988, nine out of ten agreed or strongly agreed that watching children grow up was life's greatest joy (Table 3.2). In 2002 the figure had decreased but was still a very high 81 per cent. Despite this positive evaluation, not being a parent was by no means perceived as resulting in an empty life. In the light of the growth in elective child-lessness, this is perhaps not surprising. Half of all respondents in 1988 agreed with the statement that people without children lead empty lives; this proportion more than halved by 1994, and in the most recent fielding of the question only 15 per cent held this view.

Table 3.2 *Statements about parenthood and marriage asked in 1988, 1994 and 2002 (percentage of those who agreed)*

| Statement | 1988 | 1994 | 2002 |
| --- | --- | --- | --- |
| Watching children grow up is life's greatest joy | 89 | 87 | 81 |
| People who have never had children lead empty lives | 50 | 22 | 15 |
| People who want children ought to get married | 83 | 72 | 53 |

In line with the increased tolerance of non-marital unions, a greater tolerance of non-marital parenthood also emerged. In the earliest survey, over four-fifths agreed that people who want children ought to get married, but this had dropped to just over half by 2002. In recent times, quite a positive evaluation of lone parenthood also emerged. The strongest support for this view came from women and from separated and widowed respondents. It is the case that lone-parent households tend to be headed by women: in the 1996 census, 13.4 per cent of family units were headed by a lone mother with children, compared with 2.6 per cent headed by men.

### Attitudes to Work and Family, 1988–2002

In addition to the availability of contraception, the most significant change in women's lives in the past three decades has been the proportion of women who stay in the paid labour force after marriage, or who return to the labour force after childbearing. The proportion of all women in the paid labour force stayed fairly constant in the sixty-one years from 1926 (32 per cent) to 1987 (35 per cent), growing to 54 per cent by 1999. The proportion of married women in the workforce exploded in the 1970s, and by the late 1990s was just over 50 per cent.

The major controversy that emerged when mothers began to stay in or return to the paid workforce in large numbers in the 1970s centred on the impact this would have on children and on women's 'family role'. Attitudes appear to have continued to change in Ireland over the period from 1988 to 2002, as Table 3.3 indicates.

A trend away from seeing working mothers in a negative light is strongly suggested by this data. For example, in 1988 and 1994, approx-

Table 3.3  *Statements about working mothers, asked in 1988, 1994 and 2002 (percentage of those who agreed)*

| Statement | 1988 | 1994 | 2002 |
|---|---|---|---|
| A working mother can establish just as warm and secure a relationship with her children as a mother who does not work | 55 | 62 | 60 |
| A pre-school child is likely to suffer if the mother works | 52 | 49 | 34 |
| All in all, family life suffers when the woman has a full-time job | 53 | 52 | 37 |

imately half of respondents believed that 'a pre-school child is likely to suffer if his or her mother works'. Only one-third of respondents held this view in 2002. Again, while approximately half agreed in 1988 and again in 1994 with the statement that 'All in all, family life suffers when the woman has a full-time job', the proportion dropped to 37 per cent in 2002. The trend, then, would suggest a greater acceptance of mothers in paid employment. A similarly liberal trend, albeit of a smaller magnitude, emerges in relation to people's attitudes to the quality of relationship that a working mother can have with her child. Women tend to have more liberal views than men on all three of these issues.

In 1994 and 2002, respondents were asked whether they felt that women who have children should work outside the home. Half of respondents in 1994 thought that a woman should stay at home if the child was under school age. This proportion had fallen to one-third in 2002. Also, a quarter of respondents in 1994 felt that a woman should remain at home after the youngest child starts school. This proportion had fallen to one in ten by 2002.

Overall, it is clear that traditional beliefs in these areas are changing very significantly, and in a liberal – or non-traditional – direction. With the increase in married women working outside the home, the growth of corporate culture and the long addition that commuting often makes to the working day, the issue of balancing work with home life has come to the fore in recent decades. Hochschild (1997) has suggested that the relative attractions of work and home can shift, with home becoming a more stressful place and work becoming more 'homelike'. For those in employment at the time of the 2002 study, 38 per cent described their jobs as stressful at times, while 47 per cent reported that they often had to put in extra hours at work. Nonetheless, levels of satisfaction with work were high. Of those working, and excluding those who couldn't choose a reply, 89 per cent reported themselves to be completely, very or fairly satisfied in their main job. In terms of general satisfaction with life, 43 per cent of those who responded to the question described themselves as very happy and 53 per cent were fairly happy. Two-thirds described themselves as very or completely satisfied with their home lives, while 31 per cent said they were fairly satisfied with theirs. Work was perceived to be an important source of independence for women: 61 per cent agreed that a job was the best way for a woman to be independent, with no significant variation in the views of men and women (14 per cent neither agreed or disagreed).

Additional questions were asked to focus specifically on the work–home relationship. Of those in employment, less than 20 per cent agreed with the following statement: 'I never come home from work too tired to do chores'. Nearly three in ten felt too tired several times a month, and 14 per cent felt like this several times a week. Women were more likely than men to report this tiredness. People were much less likely to arrive at work too tired to function well because of household tasks: 68 per cent said that this never happened to them. Similarly, almost two-thirds never found that family responsibilities made it difficult for them to concentrate at work; those who did were predominantly women. On the other hand, over half of respondents found that the amount of time they spent on their jobs made it difficult for them to fulfil family responsibilities at least sometimes; this was the case several times a month or more often for 16 per cent. Men were more likely than women to report that time spent at work made it difficult for them to fulfil family responsibilities. Overall, however, people were not dissatisfied with their work, as indicated above, and there were good levels of satisfaction with home life.

## Task Differentiation in Intimate Relationships, 1994–2002

Those who were living with a spouse or partner at the time of the survey were asked to indicate the way in which certain household and caring tasks were divided up in the home. This data is available for 1994 and 2002. The information on these items can be classified under a number of headings. One of these is the financial arrangements a couple make in terms of the sharing and management of income. A second is the issue of decision-making in the relationship. The third and perhaps most significant is the reporting of division of labour in the home. The last is how respondents felt about these arrangements in their relationships.

Looking first at finance, represented in Table 3.4, it emerges that the preferred option is to pool resources and 'each take out what we need'. Well over half chose this arrangement in both years. The proportion of cases where all the money was managed by one person, who then gave the partner a share, declined fairly notably from one-third in 1994 to less than a quarter in 2002. Conversely, there was an increase in those keeping their money separate, from 3 per cent in 1994 to 8 per cent in 2002. There was also a significant increase in the proportion who pooled some and kept the rest separate, from 7 per cent in 1994 to 13 per cent in 2002, perhaps indicating an increased sense that relationships may prove to be short- rather than long-term.

Table 3.4 *How spouses/partners organize household income, asked in 1994 and 2002 (percentage of those who agreed)*

| How do you organize income? | 1994 | 2002 |
|---|---|---|
| One partner manages all | 33 | 23 |
| We pool all | 58 | 56 |
| We pool some | 7 | 13 |
| We keep our money separate | 3 | 8 |

In relation to decision-making in intimate relationships, we found that in the 1994 survey, 76 per cent replied that it was always or usually the woman in the relationship who decided what to have for dinner; 23 per cent said the decision was taken jointly or with similar frequency by both. In the 2002 data, three items were asked, and considerable joint-ness was reported overall. In choosing weekend activities, the decision was either taken together (56 per cent) or was more or less interchange-able (24 per cent said 'sometimes me, sometimes my partner'). Major purchases for the home were decided on jointly by 63 per cent, and making social invitations was also characterized by jointness in a major-ity of cases (60 per cent).

The third aspect of role differentiation relates to the performance of family tasks. Questions were phrased similarly in the 1994 and 2002 sur-veys: 'In your household, who mostly does the following things?' Given the trend in a liberal direction noted earlier in this chapter, we may well expect considerable gender balance in the carrying out of everyday tasks encountered in most households. Table 3.5 suggests that we may well be disappointed.

At both time points, doing the laundry is very predominantly the preserve of the female. Regarding the preparation of meals and doing the cleaning, we only have data for 2002 but, again, these are very strongly gendered tasks. Also, in both 1994 and 2002 shopping is done by the female in the relationship for a clear majority of respondents. Caring for a sick family member is the family task in relation to which there seems to be the highest level of sharing by partners in long-term relationships, although this is still predominantly the role of women. The only task that is clearly a male preserve is doing small repairs around the house, and even here the proportion of women usually doing this task has increased (from 8 to 13 per cent between 1994 and 2002).

Table 3.5 *Performance of family tasks by sex, asked 1994–2002 (percentage of those who agreed; tasks carried out jointly not reported)*

| Tasks | Women always or usually | | Men always or usually | |
|---|---|---|---|---|
| | 1994 | 2002 | 1994 | 2002 |
| Laundry | 88 | 86 | 0 | 3 |
| Preparing meals | na | 71 | na | 6 |
| Cleaning | na | 68 | na | 3 |
| Shopping for groceries | 67 | 63 | 5 | 8 |
| Care for sick family member | 52 | 54 | 1 | 3 |
| Small repairs | 8 | 13 | 71 | 69 |

An issue looked at for the first time in 2002 was how partners feel about the share of tasks that it falls to them to do. Other research has suggested that what is salient here is not so much the numbers of hours spent on such tasks by either partner as the perceived fairness of the division of labour. Three out of five respondents disagreed with their partner on the division of household tasks at least sometimes. In the current survey, 44 per cent overall felt they did roughly their fair share. Looking at this issue more closely, it is interesting to note that women felt they did *much more* than their fair share (32 per cent) or *a bit more* than their fair share (29 per cent) (61 per cent in all); only 6 per cent of men felt like this. Thus, three in five women feel overburdened by the division of labour. However, 40 per cent of men acknowledged that they did *a bit* or *much less* than their fair share. Again, male and female perceptions are very different: 54 per cent of men compared with 36 per cent of women feel they do roughly their fair share of household tasks.

## Conclusion

It is evident from the data discussed in this chapter that change has taken place in terms of attitudes to gender roles in long-term heterosexual relationships. It has been possible to compare data on many issues from a number of time points. This comparison indicates rapidly changing views on the respective roles of adult men and women as breadwinners and house-workers. There was an expectation that both partners should contribute financially to the household; perhaps this may indicate a lack of awareness of the economic role of women within the home. Allied with the continuing predominantly female nature of the houseworker role, the additional expectation of a financial role suggests a double burden for many women. The perception of mothers as workers outside the home tended to be favourable. Women in particular tended to reject negative belief statements about the impact on home and family of mothers working outside the home.

While attitudes to family and parenthood continued to be positive, neither marriage nor children were seen as essential to happiness or a fulfilled life. Rather ominously, perhaps, women and married people in general were least likely to hold positive views of the happiness to be found in marriage. Traditional attitudes to cohabitation and divorce also underwent change, becoming increasingly tolerant. It may be of interest, however, that substantial minorities did not feel able to express a view in relation to such issues as marriage as a source of happiness, the desirability of a couple living together before marriage, long-term cohabitation, or divorce. This may reflect a loss of certainty in relation to moral issues that was much less characteristic of earlier times.

Support for mothers working outside the home is fairly strong. In practice, a fairly high proportion of mothers in the sample stayed at home when they had young children, and the strong preference when there is a child under school age in the home is to stay at home or to work only part-time. This may, of course, be related to the notorious difficulty of getting adequate childcare for working parents.

It is clear that, while there is rapid attitudinal change in progress, household gender roles in long-term heterosexual relationships are changing much less significantly, and the expectation of women as house-workers is now allied to an expectation of female economic activity outside the home. Over half of married women work outside the home, and yet continue to bear the major responsibility for all household tasks except small repair jobs in the home. In the absence of a commensurate change in the household role of men, women in long-term relationships are, in fact, working harder than they have ever done.

# References

Anderson, M. (1980), *Approaches to the History of the Western Family 1500–1914*. London: Macmillan.

Arensberg, C., and S. Kimball (1940/2001), *Family and Community in Ireland*. Cambridge, MA: Harvard University Press.

Bales, R. F., and P. E. Slater (1956), 'Role Differentiation in Small Groups', in T. Parsons and R. F. Bales (eds.), *Family: Socialization and*

*Interaction Process*. London: Routledge and Kegan Paul.

Barker, D., and S. Allen (1976), *Dependence and Exploitation in Work and Marriage*. London: Longman.

Bernard, J. (1973), *The Future of Marriage*. London: Souvenir Press.

Bernardes, J. (1985), 'Do We Really Know What The Family Is?', in P. Close and R. Collins (eds.), *Family and Economy in Modern Society*. London: Macmillan.

Boh, K. et al. (1989), *Changing Patterns of European Family Life*. London: Routledge.

Delphy, C., and D. Leonard (1992), *Familiar Exploitation: A New Analysis of Marriage in Contemporary Western Societies*. Cambridge: Polity.

Edgell, S. R. (1980), *Middle Class Couples*. London: Allen and Unwin.

Fahey, T. (1992), 'Housework, the Household Economy and Economic Development in Ireland since the 1920s', *Irish Journal of Sociology* 2: 42–69.

Fahey, T., and H. Russell (2001), 'Family Formation in Ireland'. Dublin: Economic and Social Research Institute.

Harris, C. (1983), *The Family and Industrial Society*. London: Allen and Unwin.

Hochschild, A. (1997), *The Time Bind*. New York: Henry Holt.

Morgan, D. H. J. (1975), *Social Theory and the Family*. London: Routledge and Kegan Paul.

Oakley, A. (1974), *The Sociology of Housework*. London: Martin Robertson.

Oakley, A. (1976), *Housewife*. Harmondsworth: Pelican.

O'Hara. P. (1994), 'Out of the Shadows: Women on Family Farms and their Contribution to Agriculture and Rural Development', in L. van der Plus and M. Fonte (eds.), *Rural Gender Studies in Europe*. Netherlands: Van Gorcum.

Pahl, J. M., and R. E. Pahl (1971), *Managers and their Wives*. Harmondsworth: Penguin.

Parsons, T., and R. F. Bales (eds.) (1956), *Family: Socialization and Interaction Process*. London: Routledge and Kegan Paul.

Young, M. and P. Willmott (1973), *The Symmetrical Family*. London: Routledge and Kegan Paul.

# 4. Understanding Irish Attitudes to Poverty and Wealth

*Niamh Hardiman, Tony McCashin and Diane Payne*

Inequalities in the distribution of income and wealth are a feature of all societies. Comparative studies suggest that among the developed economies income inequality is most pronounced in the USA and Switzerland. Income is much more equally distributed in Scandinavian countries and in Japan. Ireland appears to be located among those countries with relatively high levels of inequality in the distribution of income and wealth (Atkinson, 1995; Nolan and Maitre, 2000). Moreover, income inequality in Ireland increased during the 1990s and early 2000s. Three key indicators capture the reality of persistent inequality in this context of recently acquired prosperity. First, the distribution of income between wages and profits shifted markedly towards profit (Lane 1998: 225). The share of profits in the non-government sector of the economy rose from a quarter to one-third from the late 1980s to the mid-1990s and the corresponding share of wages fell from 75 per cent to 65 per cent. Secondly, among employees there was a marked rise in earnings dispersion: the ratio of the pay of the highest-paid employees to the lowest-paid rose significantly from 1987 to 1997 (Barrett et al., 1999). Finally, relative income poverty (defined as half of average disposable income) rose during the 1990s: just under 19 per cent of households were under the poverty line in 1994 and almost 26 per cent were under the poverty line in 2001 (Nolan et al., 2002: 19).

Inequality is obviously only one aspect of the 'Celtic Tiger' story, however. While inequality rose, people at all income levels were better off in absolute terms too. Employment grew at an unprecedented rate and full employment was achieved by the end of the 1990s. Earned income also rose, and this growth in earnings, when compounded by reduced taxation, resulted in a substantial rise in disposable incomes at all levels in the income distribution. The growth in employment was not confined to part-time, atypical or unskilled work: on the contrary, a substantial element of occupational upgrading took place, with an expansion in professional, managerial and ancillary employments (O'Connell, 2000). One aspect of the labour market boom was that many long-term unemployed persons found work and, as a result, entire households in which no adults had been in work during the late 1980s and early 1990s now found employment. Women thus also increased their participation in paid work. Over the period 1992 to 2002 the real value of the non-contributory old age pension increased by 39 per cent and the real value of unemployment payments increased by 33 per cent (McCashin, 2004). Absolute, as opposed to relative, poverty fell very substantially from 17 per cent in 1994 to 3 per cent in 2000 (Nolan et al., 2002).

This paper is concerned with the attitudes of Irish people to poverty and inequality.[1] We begin by elaborating the different theoretical perspectives on the causes of inequality and deprivation, focusing on the 'societal' and 'individualistic' interpretations. Then we use evidence from the ISPAS 2002 Survey to describe Irish citizens' attitudes to poverty and wealth and assess whether people are, on balance, more likely to blame poverty on social structures or on the poor themselves. Next, we explore the social bases of attitudes: what kind of people tend to blame poverty on the poor and what kind of people tend to blame social structural factors? Finally, we explore the overlap between the social and individualist interpretations and tease out the complexity of citizens' attitudes.

## Irish Attitudes to Poverty and Wealth

The most commonly applied framework in analysing attitudes to poverty is one that distinguishes between 'individualist' and 'societal' interpretations. Poverty, according to an individualist point of view, is caused by people's own actions and behaviour – their lack of motivation or hard

---

1. Few members of large modern societies, apart from expert analysts, tend to have any clear understanding of the overall patterns of income distribution that characterize the society they live in. Notwithstanding this, the attitudes of citizens to inequalities of income and wealth may well be of considerable political interest. Citizens as voters can choose among competing policy positions and opt for those that best match their own perceptions, values and attitudes. But these values and attitudes are themselves shaped by features of the society around them. For example, Svallforss (1997) found that attitudes towards the politics of redistribution are patterned according to the type of welfare system they live in – attitudes are more favourable in countries in which people already experience greater redistribution. Similarly, Rothstein (1998) found widespread support for state intervention policies among all social classes in Sweden, on a more extensive scale than in other European countries, which he attributes to widely shared positive evaluations of the Swedish welfare state. Van Oorschot and Halman (2000), analysing a wider range of countries, including postcommunist and developed market societies, found that in the market-oriented USA, with its small welfare state, individualistic assessments of inequality tended to predominate. They also found differences in the association between people's attitudes to inequality and their assessment of the state's role, with higher levels of support for the welfare state in the Nordic countries, where it was already generous, and lower levels in the 'Latin countries', with their less well-developed welfare states.

work, for example. Societal perceptions attribute poverty to broad structural factors such as lack of opportunity, discrimination against particular groups, and so on. Likewise, an individualist understanding of wealth will see it as the outcome of effort and talent and hard work, while a societal attitude will ascribe it to inherited advantage or unequal access to money and influence. This individualist–societal distinction can be understood as a continuum or scale, with strongly individualist attitudes at one end of the scale and strongly societal attitudes at the other.

The distinction between individualist and societal interpretations tends to be associated with a left–right continuum in many countries: people on the left will tend to blame society for poverty and people on the right will blame poor people themselves. However, Irish people, when asked to place themselves on a left–right scale, cluster disproportionately towards the centre–right (Laver, 1992; Hardiman and Whelan, 1994, 1998). Support for the political left in Ireland is uniquely weak in European terms (Mair, 1992; Laver, 1992, 2001). This might lead us to expect low levels of support for societal interpretations of poverty. On the other hand, Ireland's weak left may be a poor guide to underlying social attitudes, because the two main parties, Fianna Fáil and Fine Gael, are not easy to place in left–right terms, and both tend to draw electoral support from across the social spectrum. People with societal interpretations of poverty and wealth may well be voting for parties that are not 'left' in the conventional sense.

Attachment to Catholicism has been another long-standing feature of Irish political culture. But as Tony Fahey has pointed out, Catholicism might engender quite diverse interpretations (Fahey, 1992). A traditional view grounded in notions of charity is still widely expressed in the social practice and activities of Catholic charitable organizations such as the St Vincent de Paul Society. But some Catholic organizations advance distinctly radical and structural analyses of poverty. Thus, there may not be a simple link between Catholicism and attitudes to poverty and wealth. Besides, adherence to religious practice has been in rapid decline in Ireland in recent times.

Joseph Lee (1989) identified begrudgery as a central element in Irish people's sense of the social world, that is, a resentment of anyone who has achieved success and a tendency to belittle them. While based in no small measure on envy, begrudgery denies the legitimacy of public approbation of successful people. This analysis clearly had a resonance in earlier decades when Ireland had a closed economy and a culturally uniform society. This was a context in which the absolute number of opportunities for employment, social advancement and business success was small. Success for one person would mean failure for another. But the burgeoning of economic opportunity in the 1990s clearly altered the context that Lee described.

We might expect that people's attitudes would be affected to some degree not only by their objective circumstances but also by public and political discourses. Once again, we find that there is no single dominant trend in recent political debates. On the one hand, the US model of individual enterprise, low taxes, and an individualist, work-oriented philosophy was strongly supported by successive governments. On the other hand, distributive issues were kept on the policy agenda, and all governments have been committed to anti-poverty targets. More generally, revelations about political corruption are likely to have increased scepticism about how the system works and what it takes to get ahead.

Taking these broad background factors together, we might well expect that individualist and societal value-orientations could be identified in Irish society as they have been in other economically developed societies. With regard to poverty, we might distinguish between people who blame the individual on the one hand, holding that lack of enterprise or personal responsibility is at the base of their condition, and people who blame social conditions on the other, that is, blaming structural impediments for the inability of poor people to improve their situation. Similarly, with regard to people's attitudes towards wealth, we might distinguish between an individualistic and a societal explanation. People might attribute success to individuals' own hard work, initiative and merit. Or they might consider that wealth is based on the ability to manipulate a system that is unfairly rigged or that requires prior possession of social advantages and connections.

Of course, people might adopt *both* perspectives – individualist and societal – simultaneously. It is entirely possible to think that individual responsibility is vitally important to bettering one's circumstances, but that poor people start with significant disadvantages and that the playing field is far from level. It is possible to think that individual wealth is deserved on grounds of talent, effort and even luck, but that some find it easier to attain than others by virtue of the social advantages with which they start. People's attitudes, in short, may be complex and not easily amenable to classification along a single left–right/individualist–societal scale.

Furthermore, we would expect people's attitudes to poverty, wealth and inequality to be formed not only by their general values and beliefs but also by their lived, everyday experiences. Sociological studies of class (Goldthorpe et al., 1969, Sennett and Cobb, 1972) show, for example, how people can internalize one set of beliefs and also support attitudes that seem at variance with these beliefs. The actual circumstances that people encounter, and the contrasts that people may experience between general beliefs and daily life, can give rise to what have been variously described as 'compartmentalized beliefs' or 'divided selves'. People may actively accommodate a range of beliefs by forming composite explanations of poverty and wealth.

Ireland's recent economic transformation presents an intriguing context in which to analyse people's attitudes, and poses a range of questions about how it has affected public attitudes. One line of reasoning might suggest that general economic success has brought widespread adherence to a culture of entrepreneurship, a belief that individual effort and talent will bring success and that, in today's Ireland, poverty can only be due to a lack of effort. For young people in particular this set of views might accord more closely with the recent reality of full employment and rising living standards. Full employment and general prosperity has been the uninterrupted experience of younger cohorts in the population – those who embarked on work and business in the last decade or so.

Alternatively, the recent prosperity may have disturbed established points of comparison and created higher expectations, and the new-found and very visible wealth could arguably have sharpened people's sense of grievance. It is plausible that rising living standards led the population as a whole – including those on lower incomes who also experienced significant increases in income – to discount structural forces and to see poverty and wealth in individualist terms. But will the persistent inequality that we noted earlier also shape people's views? To what extent will the direct experience of business success, of moving from unemployment to work, of rising property values, of memories and experiences of past unemployment and poverty, be more likely to affect attitudes?

Existing studies of attitudes towards poverty and wealth suggest the kinds of patterns that might be found in the Irish case. Our approach was informed by the work of the International Social Justice Project (ISJP) (Kluegel et al., 1995; Marshall et al., 1997; see also van Oorschoot, 2000). The comparative analysis emanating from this work indicates that attitudes to poverty and wealth are actually structured along *two* dimensions: separate sets of individualist and societal interpretations co-exist in the population, and these form separate and independent sets of beliefs. This is consistent with the intuition outlined above, that people may value personal responsibility and initiative, but also recognize that they live in unequal societies. However, there are important variations in these perceptions. People in all social classes attach importance to individualist explanations of both poverty and wealth: there is very wide agreement that poverty is due to lack of effort and wealth to hard work, talent and so on. However, comparative studies find variation in the importance attached to societal factors in accounting for either poverty or wealth, according to the class position of their respondents. People in lower social classes are significantly more inclined to attach importance to social factors in explaining poverty or wealth, and more likely to record negative individualist accounts of wealth (wealth is due to dishonesty, for example).

## Survey Evidence on Attitudes to Poverty and Wealth

Respondents were asked to either agree or disagree with a range of statements relating to the issues of poverty and wealth (see Table 4.1). Looking first at the items on poverty, we see that all the statements offer quite negative interpretations of poverty. Agreement with these statements broadly suggests agreement with an underlying argument that individuals are responsible for their own impoverished circumstances. Disagreement with the statements seems to suggest a kind of fatalistic view: the individuals are poor because they are unlucky. The results for items 2 and 4 are particularly interesting, showing a high level of agreement with the idea that effort and hard work determines one's circumstances. These results suggest a strongly individualist perception of the poor and their predicament. Equally significantly, however, there is substantial dis-

Table 4.1 *Perceptions of poverty and wealth at the individual level*

|  | Disagree (%) | Neither agree/ disagree (%) | Agree (%) |
|---|---|---|---|
| **Perceptions of poverty** | | | |
| The people who are badly off just waste the money they have | 62.3 | 10.8 | 26.9 |
| Some people don't make the effort to help themselves | 16.5 | 6.7 | 76.8 |
| There is no real poverty left now | 75.7 | 5.6 | 18.7 |
| Hard work is what makes the difference between making a lot of money and making very little | 24.6 | 6.5 | 68.9 |
| **Perceptions of wealth** | | | |
| Everybody has an equal chance to get on | 44.2 | 4.6 | 51.2 |
| People with talent or ability will always make money | 26.8 | 7.1 | 66.1 |
| Everybody gets rewarded for their effort and hard work | 53.8 | 6.0 | 40.2 |
| Everybody in Ireland is much better off now than five years ago | 17.9 | 6.2 | 75.9 |
| If a child from a low–income family gets a good education, he or she will get on as well as any other child | 13.1 | 3.7 | 83.2 |

Table 4.2 *Attitudes to wealth and poverty at the societal level*

| | Disagree (%) | Neither agree/ disagree (%) | Agree (%) |
|---|---|---|---|
| **Attitudes to poverty** | | | |
| The government does not give enough money to people on social welfare | 34.8 | 16.3 | 48.9 |
| Great differences in wealth and income are unfair | 31.9 | 15.6 | 52.5 |
| There is one law for the rich and one for the poor | 22.8 | 5.5 | 71.7 |
| The poor are getting left behind | 24.8 | 8.1 | 67.1 |
| The ordinary person's income is not much better than five years ago | 51.3 | 8.3 | 40.4 |
| You can't really have equal opportunities because in the end it all comes down to what social class you are from | 48.6 | 8.9 | 42.5 |
| **Attitudes to wealth** | | | |
| The incomes of well-off people are rising faster than anyone else's | 7.1 | 9.4 | 83.5 |
| The only people who can make a lot of money are the people with the right connections | 43.1 | 6.9 | 50.0 |
| To become really well off you have to have some money to begin with | 33.8 | 6.1 | 60.1 |
| You have to be dishonest to make a lot of money | 75.2 | 6.0 | 18.8 |
| Ordinary workers and their families don't have the same opportunities as well-off people | 22.3 | 6.5 | 71.2 |

agreement with the statement that the poor 'just waste the money they have'. Likewise there is also strong disagreement with the statement that 'there is no real poverty left now'. Taken together, the results for the latter two items suggest that there is limited evidence of a judgemental, moralizing attitude to people who are badly off. Approximately a quarter of the population agrees with these statements. Therefore, while the population at large emphasizes the role of effort and work, it does not seem to view the lifestyle of the poor in a harsh, judgemental way.

The responses to three of the five statements relating to perceptions of wealth – the items on talent/ability, everyone being better off, and education – demonstrated high levels of agreement with the individualist interpretation. However, there was much more limited support for the statement that 'everybody gets rewarded for their effort and hard work' –

only 40 per cent agreed with this statement – and there was an almost even split as to whether 'everybody has an equal chance to get on'.

Table 4.2 presents the proportion of respondents who agreed with societal interpretations of wealth and poverty. The results suggest that there is moderate to strong agreement with this kind of explanation. Three of the items commanded agreement levels in excess of 70 per cent, and the statement that the 'incomes of well-off people are rising faster than anyone else's' secured over 80 per cent support. However, while people seem to differentiate between well-off people, poor people and ordinary people, they do not express agreement with items that explicitly point to class distinctions in society as the mechanism creating poverty and wealth. There was clearly a divided view, for example, on the item suggesting that 'it all comes down to class', with 43 per cent indicating agreement. There was weak support for statements such as 'great differences in wealth and income are unfair' and 'the ordinary person's income is not much better than five years ago'. This suggests that people clearly distinguish between those living in real poverty and the 'ordinary person', whose income is perceived to have improved during the 'Celtic Tiger' period.

Just as the individualist items did not invoke moralistic judgements of the poor, the societal items do not suggest that there is a generally negative perception of wealthy people. Fewer than 20 per cent agreed that dishonesty is a precondition for making 'a lot of money'. Likewise, there was only mixed support for the argument that 'the only people who can make a lot of money are the people with the right connections'. This suggests that while people may perceive inequalities in income distribution as a societal or systemic phenomenon, they also reject the idea that this is the result of actions by any particular group of dishonest individuals.

Taking all the items in Table 4.2 together, they suggest that while there is broad agreement about the inequitable nature of the system of income distribution in Ireland, people also understand the real losers in this system to be those living in poverty in Irish society. For example, over two-thirds of respondents agreed that 'the poor are getting left behind'. In contrast, everyone else's income was perceived to have risen, including that of the 'ordinary person', whose income has improved but not at the same pace as 'well-off people'. This may suggest some support for a kind of fatalistic view of poverty in Irish society, where people remain poor because they are unlucky enough to be living under this particular system of income distribution.[2]

---

2. Before turning to the underlying dimensions of people's attitudes, one point should be noted about the link between the items reported above and socio-economic status. We cross-tabulated the items by socio-economic status (data not given here) and the results are somewhat similar to the 'split consciousness' pattern reported by Kluegel (1995) and his colleagues.

## Dimensions of Attitudes to Poverty and Wealth

In the previous section, we reported the responses across two different sets of items on wealth and poverty. We suggested earlier that beliefs about poverty may be multi-dimensional, specifically that beliefs may reflect both individualist and societal components. In order to establish whether each of the two sets of survey items just described are indeed identifying an underlying attitudinal dimension, we used factor analysis to examine all the 20 items listed in Tables 4.1 and 4.2 above. We expected to find that the individualist items would load on one factor, while the societal items would load on a separate factor. And indeed, the results of factor analysis (see Appendix 4A) confirm the presence of the two underlying dimensions, a societal explanation factor and an individualist explanation factor.[3] Having established the existence of two dimensions underlying our attitudinal data, we then aggregated each set of items to create two new summated scales.[4] Finally, we transformed the two new summated scales and collapsed each into two categories to indicate a tendency towards either weak or strong agreement with the underlying explanation.

---

On the one hand, support for individualist items is very widespread. On the other, those in lower socio-economic groups, while supporting an individualist stance, were more likely to adopt social interpretations of poverty and negative interpretations of wealth. These differences between socio-economic groups were statistically significant, although the actual magnitude of the differences between socio-economic groups was modest.

3. Before proceeding to analyse the scaled data, there are two points that should be noted. First, although we have identified two separate dimensions, it is also not unreasonable to expect that these dimensions may be conceptually linked. The Pearson correlation between the two non-transformed scales (-0.137, significant at 0.01 level) suggests that there is some evidence of weak correlation between the underlying dimensions. Secondly, we need to acknowledge the possibility that the factors we identified (and the scales we constructed) are an artefact of the data. In particular, we were concerned that the results of our factor analysis were a function of the question direction. However, we suspect that if this was indeed a problem, we should find a much higher level of correlation of the items, as well as similar levels of agreement/disagreement across items, which was not the case in our results (see Tables 4.3 and 4.4). We also wondered whether we could observe a single underlying dimension that could combine people's perceptions of the causes of poverty and wealth, so that at one end we might expect agreement around individualistic causes of poverty and wealth, and at the other, agreement around societal causes for wealth and poverty. In our factor analysis (and tests for reliability) we examined a range of different combinations of items (including small subsets of items). However, there was no evidence to support a single underlying dimension solution.

4. The Cronbach Alpha measure for each scale exceeds 0.7, suggesting highly reliable scales.

## Profiling Respondents

Having established that there are, in fact, two dimensions to the value orientations we are interested in, individualist and societal, the next step in our discussion is to see if there is any pattern to holding these views, particularly with reference to demographic characteristics such as age, social class and gender. As shown in Table 4.3, and as we expect from our earlier discussion, higher proportions of those in the youngest age category demonstrated only weak agreement with the societal explanation, while in the oldest age category, the majority of the respondents (67.9 per cent) agreed with the societal level of explanation. A substantial proportion of these older respondents will already have been at or close to retirement age and likely to be increasingly dependent on the provision of various state-provided welfare schemes, including health and social services provision for older people.

Four-fifths of those who have great difficulty making ends meet strongly agreed with the societal explanation. Two-thirds of employees who normally have no supervisory role in the workplace supported the societal explanation of inequality, as did nearly three-quarters of those who had had recent experience of unemployment. The results for the unemployment experience and subjective economic position variables

Table 4.3 *Support for the societal level of explanation by respondent characteristics*

| Respondent characteristics | Weak agreement (%) | Strong agreement (%) |
| --- | --- | --- |
| *Age* | | |
| 16–34 | 45.3 | 54.7 |
| 35–54 | 38.7 | 61.3 |
| 55 plus | 32.1 | 67.9 |
| *Able to make ends meet. . .* | | |
| with great difficulty | 19.7 | 80.3 |
| with some difficulty | 31.6 | 68.4 |
| fairly easily | 41.3 | 58.7 |
| very easily | 57.4 | 42.6 |
| *Supervisory role* | | |
| yes | 50.8 | 49.2 |
| no | 34.4 | 65.6 |
| *Unemployment experience in last five years* | | |
| yes | 27.4 | 72.6 |
| no | 40.3 | 59.7 |

**Note:** All the results in this table are statistically significant at the .05 level or higher.

confirm the importance of quite specific, situational factors in shaping people's attitudes.

Table 4.4 *Support for the individualist level explanation by respondent characteristics*

| Respondent characteristics | Weak agreement (%) | Strong agreement (%) |
| --- | --- | --- |
| *Able to make ends meet. . .* | | |
| with great difficulty | 60.6 | 39.4 |
| with some difficulty | 43.4 | 56.6 |
| fairly easily | 42.8 | 57.2 |
| very easily | 36.4 | 63.6 |
| *Education level* | | |
| Third level | 38.3 | 61.2 |
| Secondary level or less | 55.4 | 44.6 |

Table 4.4 shows support for the individualistic explanation in terms of socio-economic characteristics. One finding that stands out is the significance of education: over 60 per cent of the respondents with a third-level qualification strongly supported the individualistic explanation, compared with fewer than half of those respondents with a secondary level of education or lower. A strongly differentiated result is also seen in support of the individualistic explanation when we look at respondents' own assessment of their economic position. Almost two-thirds (63.6 per cent) of those who experienced no financial difficulty (i.e. 'who make ends meets very easily') strongly agreed with the individualistic explanation. This compares with about the same proportion (60.6 per cent) of those who were experiencing great financial difficulty but who *disagreed* with the individualistic explanation. But while the results for the other categories of respondents examined on this characteristic are more mixed, on balance there is more rather than less support for the individualistic explanation of income inequality.

## Clusters of Attitudes

We have identified two dimensions of attitudes, an individualist and a societal dimension. In the case of the individualist scale, respondents identified in the strong category would be those who agreed with an individualist explanation of income distribution: they believed that individuals effectively determine whether they are wealthy or poor, according to how hard they work, how much talent they have, and so on. In the case of the societal scale, someone in the strong agreement category believes that the possibility of becoming wealthy or poor is largely determined by social structures and institutions, that the well-off have been doing better, and that starting out with money and connections is important.

But we also recognized that it is possible for people to hold views that do not fall entirely into one or other category. People might well have mixed values. To capture this, we need to take the information we have about how attitudes are patterned across these two dimensions and see how they interact with each other. The patterns of responses across the two scales are presented in Figure 4.1. Taking the respondents who express the strongest views on any dimension, we find quite an even pattern of distribution across the categories that might indicate the most consistent ordering of values and interpretations.

If respondents agree most strongly with the societal scale and less strongly with the individualist scale, we might consider them to have a classic 'left-wing' interpretation of wealth and poverty – that is, that while personal initiative matters, societal factors matter even more in accounting for patterns of income distribution. About a quarter of our respondents (24.4 per cent) fall into this category.

If, on the other hand, respondents agree most strongly with the individual interpretation and less strongly with the societal interpretation, we might consider these to have a classic 'liberal' interpretation of wealth and poverty – that is, while societal factors have a bearing on outcomes, individual initiative, entrepreneurship, and the free exercise of talents account for most of the outcomes in the reward structure. A little more than a quarter (28.6 per cent) of our respondents fall into this category.

Individualist explanation

|  |  | Weak support | Strong support |
|---|---|---|---|
| Societal explanation | Weak support | 14.4% | 28.6% |
| | Strong support | 24.4% | 32.7% |

Figure 4.1  *Response pattern across both explanations of income distribution*

Respondents might agree strongly with both the individualist and the societal dimension – that is, they could understand income distribution as resulting from both individualistic and societal causes. Only slightly more – about one-third of our respondents (32.7 per cent) – fall into this category. They evidently have a strong sense of individual initiative and responsibility, but also possess a strong sense of the constraints that people work under. We might consider these to fall into a 'libertarian left' category of values.

The smallest percentage of respondents – about one-seventh of the total (14.4 per cent) – is identified as being in weak agreement with both interpretations. This means that while they do not hold much truck with the notion of individuals' personal responsibility for their own situation, neither do they give much credence to explanations of poverty and wealth that are couched in terms of societal causes. These respondents may hold that people's fortunes are subject to fairly arbitrary processes that can neither be foreseen nor controlled. We might therefore term this combination of values the 'free floaters'.

## Conclusion

Our key findings are that the Irish public in general support individualist values in its interpretation of poverty and wealth, and that this stance coexists with a structural view of poverty among people in lower socioeconomic groups.

Overall, we have identified four clusters of views that may be found among the electorate. About a quarter of respondents have a value-profile that we identify as a classic left-wing position, and a little over a quarter fall into what we term a classic liberal grouping. We would expect that the former might well find parties of the left most attractive, and that the latter would be drawn to any party that stressed traditional market values. One-third of respondents take a mixed position that values individual responsibility but that also takes a wider, societal view of the conditions under which people exercise their choices. These people may well be open to persuasion by political parties stressing either of the two value orientations. The fact that the two largest parties in the Irish political system might be characterized as spanning both value orientations may help explain why this is the largest single grouping we found. Finally, the smallest grouping does not take a very strong view on either the individualist or the societal value dimension. We have termed them 'free floaters'; they may well be people with relatively little interest in politics in any case.

Examining the values and attitudes people adopt towards income inequality may help us to understand better why voters prefer some policies over others on issues relating to the distribution of wealth. Just as income inequality has increasingly been mapped comparatively, it may be of interest to understand whether there are systematic comparative differences in citizens' attitudes towards poverty and wealth, and how these can be explained. But more importantly perhaps, this kind of study may also have implications for practical politics. Mapping the cultural values underlying people's current political attitudes might make it possible to identify repertoires for future political action. Information about people's value profiles might be just as valuable to those favouring market solutions to social problems as to those interested in political interventions to redress inequalities.

We have shown some preliminary findings in this paper that indicate that the profile of Irish attitudes can be understood in terms that have already been widely identified in cross-national research. But much more needs to be done to fill in our understanding of the implications of these findings for the dynamics of party competition and political life more generally in Ireland. We intend to address these issues in future research.

## References

Atkinson, A. B., L. Rainwater and T. M. Smeeding (1995), 'Income Distribution in OECD Countries: Evidence from the Luxembourg Income Study'. Paris: OECD.

Barrett, A., J. Fitzgerald and B. Nolan (1999), 'Earnings Inequality, Returns to Education and Labour Market Institutions', *British Journal of Industrial Relations* 371: 77–100.

Fahey, T. (1992), 'Catholicism and Industrial Society in Ireland', in J. H. Goldthorpe and C. T. Whelan (eds.) (1992), *The Development of Industrial Society in Ireland*. Oxford: Clarendon Press: 241–63.

Goldthorpe, J. H., D. Lockwood, F. Bechhofer and J. Platt (1969), *The Affluent Worker: Political Attitudes and Behaviour*. Cambridge: Cambridge University Press.

Hardiman, N., and C. T. Whelan. (1994), 'Values and Political Partisanship', in Christopher T. Whelan (ed.), *Values and Social Change in Ireland*. Dublin: Gill and Macmillan.

Hardiman, N., and C. T. Whelan. (1998), 'Changing Values', in W. Crotty and D. Schmitt (eds.), *Ireland and the Politics of Change*. Harlow: Addison Wesley Longman.

Kluegel, J. R., G. Csepeli, T. Kolosi, A. Orkény and M. Neményi (1995), 'Accounting for the Rich and the Poor: Existential Justice in Comparative Perspective', in D. S. Mason and Bernd Wegener (eds.), *Social Justice and Political Change*. New York: Aldine de Gruyter.

Lane, P. (1998), 'Profits and Wages in Ireland', *Journal of the Statistical and Social Inquiry Society of Ireland* 1997/1998, XXVII.V: 223–47.

Laver, M. (1992), 'Are Irish Parties Peculiar?', in J. H. Goldthorpe and C. T. Whelan (eds.), *The Development of Industrial Society in Ireland*. Oxford: Clarendon Press/British Academy.

Laver, M. (ed.) (2001), *Estimating the Policy Positions of Political Actors*.

London: Routledge/ECPR.

Laver, M., and I. Budge (eds.) (1992), *Party Policy and Government Coalitions*. Basingstoke: Macmillan.

Lee, J. (1989), *Ireland 1912–1985*. Cambridge: Cambridge University Press.

Mair, P. (1992), 'Explaining the Absence of Class Politics in Ireland', in J. H. Goldthorpe and C. T. Whelan (eds.), *The Development of Industrial Society in Ireland*. Oxford: Clarendon Press.

McCashin, A. (2004), *Social Security in Ireland*. Dublin: Gill and Macmillan.

Marshall, G., S. Adam and S. Roberts (1997), *Against the Odds? Social Class and Social Justice in Industrial Societies*. Oxford: Clarendon Press.

Nolan, B., and B. Maitre (2000), 'Income Inequality', in B. Nolan, P. J. O'Connell and C. T. Whelan (eds.), *Bust to Boom? The Irish Experience of Growth and Inequality*. Dublin: ESRI/IPA.

Nolan, B., B. Gannon, R. Layte, D. Watson, C. T. Whelan and J. Williams (2002), *Monitoring Poverty Trends: Results from the Living in Ireland Surveys*. Dublin: ESRI.

O'Connell, P. (2000), 'The Dynamics of the Irish Labour Market in Comparative Perspective', in B. Nolan, P. J. O'Connell and C. T. Whelan (eds.), *Bust to Boom? The Irish Experience of Growth and Inequality*. Dublin: ESRI/IPA: 58–89.

Rothstein, B. (1998), *Just Institutions Matter: The Moral and Political Logic of the Universal Welfare State*. Cambridge: Cambridge University Press.

Sennett, R., and J. Cobb (1972), *The Hidden Injuries of Class*. Cambridge: Cambridge University Press.

Svallforss, S. (1997), 'Worlds of Welfare and Attitudes to Redistribution: a Comparison of Eight Western Nations', *European Sociological Review* 13.3: 283–304.

Van Oorschot, W., and L. Halman (2000), 'Blame or Fate, Individual or Social? An International Comparison of Popular Explanations of Poverty', *European Societies* 2.1: 1–28.

Appendix 4A *Rotated pattern and structure matrices*

| Survey Items | Item Labels | Pattern matrix Social Individualist Factor | Factor | Structure matrix Social Individualist Factor | Factor |
|---|---|---|---|---|---|
| The only people who can make a lot of money are the people with the right connections | C1.2 | 0.65 | | 0.643 | |
| You can't really have equal opportunities because in the end it all comes down to what social class you are from | C6.5 | 0.615 | | 0.616 | |
| The incomes of well-off people are rising faster than anyone else's | C5.3 | 0.516 | | 0.515 | |
| To become really well off you have to have to start off with some money | C1.5 | 0.497 | | 0.491 | |
| Great differences in wealth and income are unfair | C7.4 | 0.481 | | 0.484 | |
| The poor are getting left behind | C5.2 | 0.475 | | 0.475 | |
| There is one law for the rich and one for the poor | A3.4 | 0.468 | | 0.472 | |
| The government does not give enough money to people on social welfare | C1.4 | 0.465 | | 0.470 | |
| You have to be dishonest to make a lot of money | C1.9 | 0.456 | | 0.453 | |
| Ordinary workers and their families don't have the same opportunities as well-off people | C6.3 | 0.441 | | 0.452 | |

Appendix 4A *Continued*

| Survey Items | Item Labels | Pattern matrix | | Structure matrix | |
|---|---|---|---|---|---|
| | | Social Factor | Individualist Factor | Social Factor | Individualist Factor |
| The ordinary person's income is not much better than five years ago | C5.4 | 0.439 | | 0.447 | |
| Everybody has an equal chance to get on | C6.1 | | 0.673 | | 0.683 |
| Everybody gets rewarded for their effort and hard work | C6.2 | | 0.651 | | 0.656 |
| Everybody in Ireland is much better off now than five years ago | C5.1 | | 0.581 | | 0.584 |
| People with talent always make money | C1.6 | | 0.552 | | 0.544 |
| There is no real poverty left now | C5.5 | | 0.542 | | 0.536 |
| Badly off people just waste their money | C1.1 | | 0.520 | | 0.507 |
| Hard work makes the difference between a lot of money and a little | C1.7 | | 0.486 | | 0.483 |
| If a child from a low-income family gets a good education, he or she will get on as well as any other child | C6.4 | | 0.377 | | 0.390 |
| Some people don't make the effort to help themselves | C1.3 | | 0.367 | | 0.367 |

**Note**: Extraction method: Principal Component Analysis/Rotation Method: Oblimin with Kaiser Normalization/Cumulative Extraction sums of squared loadings: 29.3%.

# 5. Political Alienation

## John Garry

The issue of political alienation has preoccupied Irish, as well as international, politicians and commentators for some time. Concerns are regularly voiced about the quality of Irish democracy and the apparently large number of citizens who are disengaged from and uninterested in politics. The most obvious focus for such concerns is the increasingly large proportion of the electorate that does not turn out to vote in our various elections (general, local and European) and referendums (on the issues of the EU and abortion, for example) (Lyons and Sinnott, 2003). Low turnouts are typically viewed as the result of an apathetic and cynical electorate who either do not care about politics or do not see enough difference between the parties on offer to make voting for any of them worthwhile.

Furthermore, cynicism about politics will certainly not have been lessened by the seemingly endless round of tribunals of inquiry into alleged political wrongdoing in recent years. The McCracken, Flood and Moriarty tribunals (to name but three) have highlighted, among other things, allegations of improper payments to politicians, dodgy dealings over land re-zoning and wrongful spending by a former Taoiseach on very expensive Charvet shirts (Murphy, 2003). It is small wonder, therefore, that many citizens feel unimpressed with politics and politicians and feel alienated from the political system.

'Political alienation' is a term widely used in the academic literature to describe the negative attitudes that many citizens have towards the political system. The concept of alienation is made up of a number of components: trust, efficacy, interest and knowledge.[1] Political trust may be seen as a general sense of support for, or confidence in, the political system and political leaders. Easton, for example, states that '. . . the presence of trust would mean that [citizens] would feel that their own interests would be attended to even if the authorities were exposed to

---

1. For a discussion of the various components or dimensions of the concept of alienation see, for example, Finifer (1970) and Southwell (1985).

little supervision or scrutiny' (1975: 447). In other words, people who trust politicians and the political system feel that the natural inclination of those in power is to behave properly and not simply in their own self-ish interests. Gabriel (1995: 361) describes the notion of political trust as follows:

> Political leaders are trusted because they are perceived as open minded, fair, responsive and acting in the best interests of the political community. In contrast, cynics think of political leaders as elitist, corrupt, unresponsive, and primarily intent on pursuing their own interests or benefiting a narrow segment of the public. In the long run, distrust of political leaders may become generalized and eventually attributed to political institutions and processes.

Several authors have emphasized that moderate levels of trust in politics is necessary for a healthy democracy. Iglitzin (1972: 48) states that confidence in the system 'engenders peaceful and willing support for the system'. He issues a dire warning about the impact of high levels of mistrust: '...but when confidence changes to apathy, mistrust, and cynicism, little is required to convert these attitudes into uncontrolled behaviour'. Similarly, Dahl argues that trust is a necessary prerequisite for a healthy democracy because it facilitates mutual communication, makes it possible to organize to promote citizens' aims and makes conflict easier to address and manage.[2]

In addition to mistrusting politics and the political system, politically alienated citizens also tend to have low 'political efficacy'. In other words, they feel politically incompetent or ineffective; they do not understand politics very well and believe that they cannot have an impact on politics because their views are not taken on board by politicians. An early definition of the notion of political efficacy can be found in Campbell et al. (1954: 187):

> The feeling that individual political action does have, or can have, an impact upon the political process, i.e. that it is worthwhile to perform one's civic duties. It is the feeling that political and social change is possible and that the individual citizen can play a part in bringing about this change.[3]

Later analysts, such as Lane (1959) and Almond and Verba (1963), have identified two distinct types of efficacy. These are sometimes called 'personal' and 'system' efficacy. The distinction here is between the extent to which a citizen feels informed about and able to understand political debate (personal efficacy) and the extent to which a citizen thinks the system responds to personal views and the views of the public (system efficacy). Citizens who have high levels of *personal* efficacy perceive

2. Dahl's argument is summarized by Cole (1973).
3. See Gabriel (1995) for a discussion of this definition.

themselves to be politically effective and competent. They feel that they are well equipped to deal with political matters and to grapple with the key national issues of the day. Citizens who are high in *system* efficacy 'believe that the political system can respond to their needs and wishes' (Bromley and Curtice, 2002: 144) and perceive the political system and government as 'open and responsive to the average citizens' demands' (Gabriel, 1995: 360).

In addition to exploring levels of trust and personal and system efficacy, I explore how interested citizens are in politics. A lack of interest in politics seems to be a very basic and useful measure of alienation. If people are extremely uninterested in politics, for whatever reasons, they are unlikely to be politically involved at any level and they will thus lie on the fringes of political debate and action. A further, and related, measure of alienation I explore relates to political knowledge. If certain citizens know very little about politics, they cannot really understand or participate in contemporary political debate and are thus effectively on the margins of political life.

Overall, *alienated* citizens are seen in this chapter as those who have little or no interest or trust in politics, know very little about it and feel that politics is a fairly pointless endeavour, since their views are unlikely to have any significant effect. 'Unalienated' or 'politically engaged' citizens, by contrast, have a fairly comprehensive knowledge of political life, are interested in politics, trust social and political institutions, feel that they comprehend politics and think that their views are likely to have an impact.

This chapter has three aims. First, I describe the levels of political alienation in Ireland today. This involves describing the responses to questions – asked in the 2002 ISPAS Survey – which tap levels of interest, trust, knowledge and efficacy. Secondly, I explore whether certain types of people are more alienated than others. For example, is political alienation related to social class? Citrin et al. elaborate on this question as follows (1975: 15):

> One frequently encounters the proposition, among both scholars and laymen, that political allegiance and alienation reflect one's level of economic status. According to this view, the 'haves' are likely to be allegiant and the 'have nots' disaffected. Groups that are disadvantaged, presumably have less of a stake in the existing order and are more likely to reject it. Thus, the contention that the higher one's income, education or occupational prestige, the more favourable one's view of the political system appears to rest on the following implicit assumptions: that being economically deprived results in feeling deprived, that economic security and advancement are highly salient values, and that the 'have nots' hold the prevailing institutions and office holders responsible for their disadvantaged situation.

Being poor, the argument goes, means being alienated in general, which means being politically alienated in particular. In addition to social class, I also investigate whether the alleged public–private distinction between the social roles for men and women is observable. Is it true that women are more associated with the domestic or private realm and are thus uninterested in and distant from politics, while 'public' man is more at ease with and knowledgeable about the political world? And, furthermore, to what extent is the commonplace assertion that young people are alienated from politics true?

The third aim of the chapter is to explore the implications of political alienation. In terms of political behaviour, do the politically alienated behave differently than the unalienated? How much less likely to vote are the alienated compared with the unalienated? Which particular components or dimensions of alienation are most strongly related to non-voting? Is support for different political parties related to levels of alienation? Are citizens who are relatively highly alienated more likely to support the newer 'non-establishment' parties (Sinn Féin and the Green Party) compared with the more traditional parties? In turn, the following sections of this chapter explore the levels of, the social bases of, and the consequences of political alienation.

## Levels of Political Alienation

How interested are people in politics? Figure 5.1 reports that the population is almost evenly divided between those reporting an interest in politics and those indicating that they do not have an interest.[4] Fifty-four per cent said that they were either very or somewhat interested and 46 per cent said they were either not very or not at all interested. It is noteworthy that the proportion who indicated that they were not at all interested was almost one-fifth of respondents and larger than those who indicated the other extreme (only 12 per cent reported that they were very interested).

To what extent do Irish citizens trust their social and political institutions? Respondents were asked to indicate on a 0–10 scale the extent to which they trusted a given institution (0 being 'do not trust at all' and 10 being 'trust a lot'). I divide this 11-point scale into three. Respondents who indicated 0, 1, 2 or 3 on the scale are regarded as being low in trust for that particular institution; respondents indicating 4, 5 or 6 are regarded as having medium levels of trust; and respondents indicat-

---

4. The results presented in the tables and figures in this chapter are based on weighted data. The Ns reported in the tables are unweighted. The N for Figure 5.1 is 2481 and for Figure 5.2 is 2330. In all analyses, missing data is excluded.

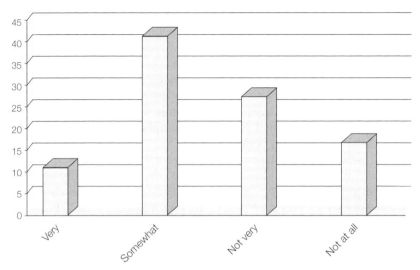

Figure 5.1  *How interested are you in politics? (%).*

ing 7, 8, 9 or 10 are regarded as being high in trust. Table 5.1 reports the overall level of trust that citizens have in the different institutions. The gárdaí emerged as being highly trusted. Only 12 per cent of respondents had low trust in the gárdaí and 59 per cent had high trust. This results in a positive balance of 47 per cent. Also highly trusted is the civil service. Only 11 per cent had low trust and 50 had high trust in the civil service (positive balance of 39 per cent). The other institution to have received high levels of trust is the courts (positive balance of 30 per cent).

By far the worst performers on this measure of trust are the mass media and political parties. Both are held in very low esteem by the public: 37 per cent had low trust in the media and 38 per cent in the political parties; and only 17 and 14 per cent respectively report high trust. These scores show that there is wide variation in the public mind over which institutions deserve trust. Political parties and the mass media clearly do not instil confidence in citizens, especially when contrasted with the legal system (gárdaí and courts) and the civil service. The results are particularly worrying for political parties. The many tribunals set up to enquire into alleged political corruption in recent years seem to have undermined confidence in political parties, and no quick fixes seem in sight. In relation to religion, about one-third of respondents trust religious leaders, while about a quarter do not. This almost certainly represents a decline in the level of trust in the religious, compared with decades gone by. But it is instructive to note that religious leaders are still the fourth most trusted of the nine institutions examined.

Table 5.1 *How much do you personally trust each of the following?*

| | %<br>Low<br>trust | %<br>Medium<br>trust | %<br>High<br>trust | % High<br>minus<br>% Low |
|---|---|---|---|---|
| Gárdaí | 12 | 28 | 59 | +47 |
| Civil service | 11 | 39 | 50 | +39 |
| Courts | 16 | 38 | 46 | +30 |
| Religious leaders | 26 | 41 | 33 | +7 |
| Business leaders | 24 | 50 | 26 | +2 |
| Government | 30 | 43 | 27 | −3 |
| Dáil | 30 | 45 | 25 | −5 |
| Mass media | 37 | 45 | 17 | −20 |
| Political parties | 38 | 47 | 14 | −24 |

Percentage of 'low trust' respondents includes those who indicated 0, 1, 2 or 3 on the 0–10 scale,. Percentage of 'medium trust' respondents includes those who indicated 4, 5 or 6. Percentage of 'high trust' respondents includes those who indicated 7, 8, 9 or 10. Numbers may not sum to 100 due to rounding.
Cases weighted by wgtall.
Lowest N = 2457.

*Source:* ISPAS 2002 (a10).

I now explore how politically 'efficacious' or 'effective' Irish people feel. As, noted, two types of efficacy are explored – 'personal' and 'system' efficacy. Personal efficacy relates to the extent to which citizens feel that they are able to understand politics and have adequate knowledge of it. Table 5.2 reports that a clear majority – 61 per cent – agreed that 'sometimes politics and government seem so complicated that a person like me cannot really understand what is going on'. A similarly clear majority – 56 per cent – disagreed with the statement: 'I think I am better informed about politics and government than most people'. These responses seem to indicate relatively low levels of personal efficacy. Only one-third *disagreed* that politics is overly complicated and only a quarter felt they were relatively well informed about politics.

In relation to system efficacy, findings are more mixed. System efficacy, as noted earlier, is the extent to which citizens feel that politics can make a difference: that the views of individuals have an impact on political outcomes, that parties offer a real choice, governments can change things and that, overall, the system works. Clear majorities – 56 and 69 per cent respectively – agreed that 'the ordinary person has no influence on politics' and that 'it doesn't really matter which political party is in power, in the end things go on much the same'. However a clear majority – even in these days of incessant talk of 'globalization' – thought that the Irish government matters. Over 60 per cent disagreed that 'in today's world, an

Table 5.2 *Levels of efficacy: percentage of respondents who agreed with the following statements*

|  | Disagree | Neither agree nor disagree | Agree | Total |
|---|---|---|---|---|
| **Personal Efficacy** | | | | |
| Sometimes politics and government seem so complicated that a person like me cannot really understand what is going on. | 33 | 6 | 61 | 100 |
| I think I am better informed about politics and government than most people. | 56 | 17 | 27 | 100 |
| **System Efficacy** | | | | |
| The ordinary person has no influence on politics. | 40 | 4 | 56 | 100 |
| It doesn't really matter which political party is in power, in the end things go on much the same. | 25 | 6 | 69 | 100 |
| In today's world, an Irish government can't really influence what happens in this country. | 62 | 9 | 28 | 99 |

Lowest N = 2473
Data weighted by wgtall.
Concept of system efficacy also includes a question on satisfaction with democracy (Figure 7.2).
Numbers may not sum to 100 due to rounding.
*Source:* ISPAS 2002 (A91, A93, A92, A95, A94).

Irish government cannot really influence what happens in this country'. There is additional positive news for the state of Irish democracy. As reported in Figure 5.2, a very large majority – 73 per cent – is either very or fairly satisfied with the way democracy works in Ireland.

Finally, levels of political knowledge were measured using a set of multiple choice questions. Respondents were asked to choose the correct answer from four alternatives (in the style of 'Who Wants to be a Millionaire'). As reported in Table 5.3, only 11 per cent could not identify Bertie Ahern as leader of Fianna Fáil. Almost 30 per cent did not correctly identify Michael Noonan as leader of the second biggest party, Fine Gael. Just over one-third correctly answered that Trevor Sargent

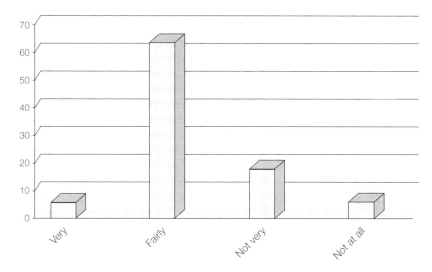

Figure 5.2 *Satisfied with the way democracy works in Ireland?*

was leader of the Green Party and that David Byrne was the Irish EU Commissioner. Less than one-fifth correctly answered the most difficult question, which asked respondents to identify Seamus Pattisson as the current Ceann Comhairle.

Table 5.3 *Political knowledge: Percentage of respondents who correctly identified the following political figures*

| | |
|---|---|
| Bertie Ahern as leader of Fianna Fáil | 89 |
| Michael Noonan as leader of Fine Gael | 72 |
| Trevor Sargent as leader of the Greens | 36 |
| David Byrne as EU Commissioner | 35 |
| Seamus Pattisson as Ceann Comhairle | 16 |

When we consider the number of knowledge questions that respondents correctly answered there is a remarkably even spread of respondents – see Table 5.4. The same proportion correctly answered none and all the questions (9 per cent). The same proportion answered one and four (17 per cent). Almost half of respondents correctly answered two or three questions correctly.

Table 5.5 offers a brief summary of levels of alienation.[5] One-third of Irish people trust only one or none of the nine social and political insti-

5. It should be emphasized that 'alienation' levels could be summarized in a variety of ways. The key reason for offering a summary such as the one offered here is that it makes the analysis that follows more straightforward and easier to interpret.

Table 5.4 *The percentage of respondents who answered each of five political knowledge questions correctly*

| | |
|---|---|
| None out of five | 9 |
| One out of five | 17 |
| Two out of five | 26 |
| Three out of five | 22 |
| Four out of five | 17 |
| Five out of five | 9 |
| Total | 100 |

tutions examined. Two-fifths of Irish people are personally inefficacious: they feel relatively poorly informed about politics and think it is too complicated for them to understand. Almost 30 per cent of respondents suffered system inefficacy: they indicated an inefficacious position on three of our four system efficacy questions. Almost half the respondents were uninterested in politics and slightly over half were able to answer only two or less of the five knowledge questions. In the following section, we relate the five elements of alienation – as operationalized in Table 5.5 – to a range of social and demographic characteristics in order to identify what types of people tend to be politically alienated.[6]

Table 5.5 *Summary of levels of political alienation*

| *Alienation dimension* | *%* |
|---|---|
| Low trust (% who indicated a high level of trust (7–10 on the 0–10 scale) in one or none of the nine institutions) | 32 |
| Low personal efficacy (% who agreed that politics is too complicated and that they felt relatively ill–informed) | 41 |
| Low system efficacy (% who indicated a low efficacy response to 3 or 4 of the 4 system efficacy questions) | 29 |
| Low interest in politics (% who indicated that they were either not very or not at all interested in politics) | 46 |
| Low knowledge (% who were only able to answer two or fewer of the five political knowledge questions) | 52 |

Lowest N = 2305

6. Appendix 5A reports correlations between the different components of alienation. Having a low level of alienation on one of the five dimensions is related to having a low level of alienation on the others. The components of alienation that are most strongly related are political knowledge, interest and personal efficacy. This is hardly surprising, since these measures tap similar things: being interested, knowing things about politics and perceiving yourself as well informed and capable in relation to politics.

## The Social Bases of Political Alienation

Is it true, following the quote from Citrin et al. cited earlier, that the 'have nots' are more likely to be politically alienated than the 'haves'? In Table 5.6 we relate social class (higher, medium or lower socio-economic groups) to alienation.[7] No relationship between class and trust emerges. However, there are big differences between the levels of efficacy, interest and knowledge found in the highest social group compared with the lowest social group. For example, only 33 per cent of people in the highest social group (the top third in terms of social class) are uninterested in politics, while 54 per cent of the lowest social group (bottom third) are uninterested. Fully 60 per cent of people in the lowest social group have low knowledge of politics compared with only 38 per cent of people in the highest social group. Respondents in the high social class group are also much more efficacious. Only a quarter of people in the high social group have low personal efficacy compared with half of the lowest social group. Similarly only a fifth of those in the highest social group have low system efficacy compared with a third in the low social class group.

Table 5.6 *Political alienation by social class (%)*.

|  | Low trust | Low personal efficacy | Low system efficacy | Low interest | Lowest knowledge | N |
|---|---|---|---|---|---|---|
| Low social class | 32 | 50 | 34 | 54 | 60 | 659 |
| Mid social class | 32 | 45 | 31 | 49 | 55 | 691 |
| High social class | 31 | 26 | 21 | 33 | 38 | 677 |

The same patterns hold for education. As reported in Table 5.7, the more educated one is, the less alienated one is. Only 29 per cent of respondents who had attended third level suffered low personal efficacy compared with 49 per cent of respondents whose highest educational qualification was the junior/inter. cert. or less. Only 19 per cent of third-level respondents suffered low system efficacy (compared with 36 per cent of the junior cert. or less group). In terms of interest, there is a 19 per cent gap between the lowest and highest educated groups and a 14 per cent gap in terms of knowledge.

7. We employ the Ganzeboom and Treiman International Socio-Economic Index (ISEI). This social class index transforms ISCO88 occupational categories into a scale according to the level of education and income associated with the different occupations. For a description of the scale see Ganzeboom and Treiman, 1992. For instructions on how to transform ISCO88 into ISEI see http://www.cf.ac.uk/socsi/CAMSIS/Data/Ireland96.html.

Table 5.7 *Political alienation by education*

|  | Low trust | Low personal efficacy | Low system efficacy | Low interest | Lowest knowledge | N |
|---|---|---|---|---|---|---|
| *Junior or less* | 33 | 49 | 36 | 55 | 58 | 983 |
| *Leaving cert.* | 30 | 44 | 29 | 44 | 52 | 580 |
| *Third level* | 33 | 29 | 19 | 36 | 44 | 736 |

Are women more alienated than men? Yes. Only 32 per cent of men but 49 per cent of women have low levels of system efficacy (Table 5.8). Also, there is a very large, 15 percentage point sex gap in relation to levels of interest in and knowledge of politics. Fifty-four per cent of women were uninterested in politics, compared with only 39 per cent of men, and 59 per cent of women had low levels of political knowledge compared with only 44 per cent of men. The public male versus private female distinction seems therefore alive and well in relation to sex differences and political alienation in modern Ireland.

Table 5.8 *Political alienation by sex*

|  | Low trust | Low personal efficacy | Low system efficacy | Low interest | Lowest knowledge | N |
|---|---|---|---|---|---|---|
| *Men* | 30 | 32 | 26 | 39 | 44 | 1044 |
| *Women* | 34 | 49 | 31 | 54 | 59 | 1259 |

Are young people more politically alienated than older people? Yes. Thirty-nine per cent of 16–34 year olds mistrust institutions, compared with only 23 per cent of 54+ year olds (see Table 5.9). The youngest age group is also more personally inefficacious than the 35–54 and 55+ age groups. The 16–34 year olds are also strikingly more uninterested in and had far lower levels of political knowledge than the two older groups. Fifty-four per cent of 16–34 year olds were uninterested in politics, compared with only 41 per cent of 35–54 year olds and 40 per cent of 55+ year olds. Similarly, two-thirds of 16–34 year olds had low levels of political knowledge compared with only 44 per cent of 35–54 year olds and 39 per cent of 55+ year olds.

Finally, in relation to religiosity there are striking differences between people who attend church frequently and infrequent church attendees. Highly religious people are more likely to trust social and political institutions and to be knowledgeable. However, they are also more likely than those who attend church infrequently to have low system efficacy (see Table 5.10).

Table 5.9 *Political alienation by age*

|  | Low trust | Low personal efficacy | Low system efficacy | Low interest | Lowest knowledge | N |
|---|---|---|---|---|---|---|
| *16–34* | 39 | 47 | 27 | 54 | 67 | 699 |
| *35–54* | 32 | 37 | 28 | 41 | 44 | 892 |
| *55+* | 23 | 37 | 31 | 40 | 39 | 702 |

Table 5.10 *Political alienation by frequency of church attendance*

|  | Low trust | Low personal efficacy | Low system efficacy | Low interest | Lowest knowledge | N |
|---|---|---|---|---|---|---|
| *Weekly or more* | 28 | 40 | 31 | 44 | 43 | 1347 |
| *Less than weekly* | 36 | 42 | 24 | 46 | 61 | 840 |

All of the social characteristics explored above are related to one or other of the components of political alienation. It is obvious, however, that the social characteristics are themselves interrelated. For example, older people tend to be more religious. Being highly educated and being in a high social class are also strongly associated. Thus, an analysis was conducted that checks whether social characteristics are *independently* related to alienation. For example, it might be that social class is most strongly related to alienation and that we only observe an education effect because education is closely related to class.

Appendix 5B reports a multivariate analysis in which all of the social characteristics are included in the same analysis to predict levels of alienation. The multivariate results confirm the findings discussed above. Even controlling for all other social characteristics, there is a strong sex effect: women are more likely than men to be alienated on all five measures of alienation, irrespective of class, education, age, urban/rural and religiosity. It is one of the top two best predictors of four of the five elements of alienation (and the third best predictor in the fifth element).[8] The effects of age, education, class, place of residence and religiosity also hold up at multivariate level. It is noteworthy that political knowledge is the element of alienation that is most strongly related to these social characteristics.[9]

8. In the multivariate analysis, scales were used rather than categorical variables, both for dependent and independent variables. Thus the findings are robust to different operationalizations of the dimensions of alienation.
9. It has the highest r-square (a measure of variation explained).

## The Consequences of Alienation: Party Choice and Turnout

How is political alienation related to party support? A question in the survey asked: 'If there was a general election tomorrow, to which party would you give your first preference vote?' The response options the respondent could choose between included the six main parties (Fianna Fáil, Fine Gael, Labour, Progressive Democrats, Green Party and Sinn Féin), plus 'independent' 'don't know' and 'I wouldn't vote'.[10]

Table 5.11 *Alienation by vote intention*

|  | *All* | *FF* | *FG* | *LAB* | *PD* | *GR* | *SF* | *IND* | *DK* | *WNV* |
|---|---|---|---|---|---|---|---|---|---|---|
| *Low knowledge* | 52 | 49* | 41+ | 47 | 24+ | 41* | 66‡ | 53 | 59+ | 86+ |
| *Low trust* | 32 | 26+ | 26‡ | 32 | 36 | 49+ | 49+ | 38 | 35 | 50+ |
| *Low interest* | 46 | 41+ | 35+ | 43 | 20+ | 50 | 41 | 47 | 56+ | 88+ |
| *Low system efficacy* | 29 | 25‡ | 26 | 38‡ | 24 | 28 | 39* | 27 | 29 | 43+ |
| *Low personal efficacy* | 41 | 41 | 33+ | 40 | 28* | 40 | 41 | 38 | 43 | 63+ |
| *Lowest N* |  | 819 | 348 | 155 | 62 | 93 | 95 | 86 | 467 | 96 |

Abbreviations: FF = Fianna Fáil; FG = Fine Gael; LAB = Labour; PD = Progressive Democrats; GR = Greens; SF = Sinn Féin; IND = Independents; DK = Don't Know; WNV = Would Not Vote
Data weighted by wgtall
* Statistically significant at .05 level
‡ Statistically significant at .01 level
+ Statistically significant at .001 level
*Source:* ISPAS (a15 and alienation variables discussed in text).

It emerges – see Table 5.11 – that Fianna Fáil supporters are much more likely than non-Fianna Fáil supporters to trust social and political institutions. Only 26 per cent of Fianna Fáil supporters are low in trust, compared with 32 per cent in the population as a whole. Fianna Fáil supporters also have relatively high levels of system efficacy and interest. Overall, Fianna Fáil supporters are not alienated. The same applies for supporters of Fine Gael and the Progressive Democrats. On four out of five measures, Fine Gael supporters are less alienated than non-Fine Gael supporters. Progressive Democrat supporters are significantly more likely than non-Progressive Democrat supporters to be interested in politics and knowledgeable about it. No clear pattern emerges for the Labour Party. Green Party and Sinn Féin supporters have a strong mis-

10. A further category, 'other', was also included in the survey but was excluded from this analysis.

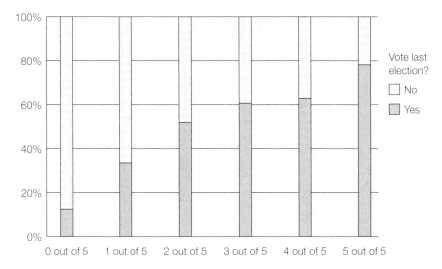

Figure 5.3 *Turnout by knowledge level*

trust of social and political institutions. Forty-nine per cent of both of these parties' supporters were low in trust compared with only 32 per cent of the population as a whole. Yet Sinn Féin and the Greens are quite different when it comes to political knowledge. The former had low levels of knowledge whereas the latter were very knowledgeable.

A range of multivariate analyses (not reported here) was also conducted to see what elements of alienation, if any, were related to party choice when all social characteristics and alienation dimensions are controlled for. The key variable that emerges is trust. Over and above the impact of social characteristics and the other elements of alienation, having relatively high levels of trust in social and political institutions is a highly statistically significant predictor of being a Fianna Fáil supporter. Having low levels of trust is a highly statistically significant predictor of being a Green Party supporter, and also of being a Sinn Féin supporter. Knowledge levels also emerge as having independent effects: high knowledge levels are statistically significantly related to voting for the Progressive Democrats and low knowledge levels are statistically significantly related to voting for Sinn Féin.

It also emerges, perhaps unsurprisingly, that responding that you 'don't know' who you would vote for is associated with being alienated. Also, the small number of respondents who said that they 'would not vote' are extremely alienated on all measures. A further question in the survey asked people if they voted in the last election (1997). Of the five measures of alienation, the best predictors of non-voting proved to be knowledge level and interest in politics. Figure 5.3 shows the level of

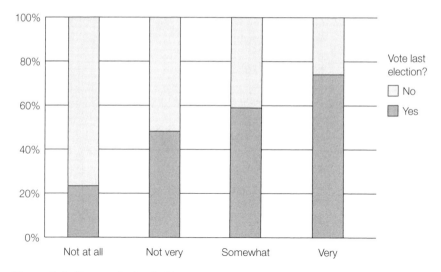

Figure 5.4 *Turnout by level of interest*

turnout for each of six political knowledge levels. Only 13 per cent of people who could not correctly answer any questions voted in the preceding election.[11] The proportion of people who turn out steadily increases as knowledge level increases. Of those who answered one question correctly, 33 per cent turned out; of those who answered two correctly, 50 per cent turned out; of those who answered three correctly, 61 per cent turned out; of those who answered four correctly, 67 per cent turned out; and 77 per cent of those who answered all five questions correctly turn out.

Figure 5.4 relates interest level to turnout and it emerges that only 24 per cent of those not at all interested in politics turn out, compared with 72 per cent of those who are very interested.

## Conclusion

In terms of levels of interest in politics and knowledge of politics, Irish citizens are relatively evenly divided. About half are not very, or not at all, interested in politics and about half are only able to answer at most two out of five knowledge questions. A wide variation emerged in terms of levels of trust in different social and political institutions. The courts, gárdaí and civil service instil confidence in people, while the media and political parties are held in very low esteem.

11. Note that this analysis excludes respondents less than 24 years old

Quite low levels of system efficacy emerged on two questions: large majorities of respondents thought that ordinary people do not have much influence on politics and that changing the political parties in power is unlikely to make much difference. However, approximately three-quarters of respondents declared themselves satisfied with democracy and a large majority still think the government has a lot of power to make a difference to people's lives. In relation to personal efficacy, the results seem more straightforward. Clear majorities indicated that they are low in personal efficacy: they felt that politics is too complicated and did not feel that they have above-average levels of information about politics.

A very clear picture emerges as to the social structure underpinning political alienation. Perhaps the most interesting result relates to the sex difference: on all five measures, and controlling for all other factors, women are more alienated than men. This seems to indicate that politics is still a man's game and men are still much more 'public' animals than women. The commonplace assumption that people from lower social groups are more likely to be alienated is confirmed. Richer people, it appears, have more to lose by not engaging with the political system, so they tend to engage. Similarly, less educated people are more likely to be alienated than educated people. There is also an interesting positive relationship between religiosity and not being alienated. It seems that regular attendance at church has an independent impact, making attendees feel engaged, interested and trusting in the system. This may be interpreted as backing Putnam's arguments (2000) on 'social capital' – that involvement and participation tend to lead to trust in the political system.

Of the five components of alienation, the most effective predictors of turnout are interest and knowledge. There are also some interesting relationships between party choice and alienation. The key finding is as follows: Fianna Fáil supporters tend to be high in political trust and Green and Sinn Féin supporters tend to be very low in trust.

## References and Bibliography

Acock, A., H. D. Clarke and M. C. Stewart (1985), 'A New Model for Old Measures: A Covariance Structure Analysis of Political Efficacy', *Journal of Politics* 47: 1062–84.

Almond, G., and S. Verba (1963), *The Civic Culture: Political Attitudes and Democracy in Five Nations*. Boston: Little, Brown.

Bromley. C., and J. Curtice (2002), 'Where Have All the Voters Gone?' in A. Park et al. (eds.), *British Social Attitudes: The 19th Report*. London: Sage.

Campbell, A., G. Gurin and W. E. Miller (1954), *The Voter Decides.* Evanston, IL: Row and Peterson.

Citrin J., H. McClosky, J. Shanks and P. Sniderman (1975), 'Personal and Political Sources of Political Alienation', *British Journal of Political Science* 5: 1–31.

Cole, R. L. (1973), 'Towards a Model of Political Trust: A Causal Analysis', *American Journal of Political Science* 17: 809–17.

Craig, S. C., R. G. Niemi and G. E. Silver (1990), 'Political Efficacy and Trust', *Political Behaviour* 12: 289–314.

Dahl, R.A. (1971), *Polyarchy.* New Haven, CT: Yale University Press.

Easton, D. (1975), 'A Re-Assessment of the Concept of Political Support', *British Journal of Political Science* 5: 435–57.

Finifer, A. W. (1970), 'Dimensions of Political Alienation', *American Political Science Review* 65: 389–410.

Ganzeboom, H., and D. Treiman (1992), 'Internationally Comparable Measures of Occupational Status for the 1988 International Standard Classification of Occupation', *Social Science Research* 25: 207–39.

Gabriel, O. W. (1995), 'Political Efficacy and Trust', in J. W. van Deth and E. Scarbrough (eds.), *The Impact of Values.* Oxford: Oxford University Press.

Iglitzin, L. B. (1972), *Violent Conflict in American Society.* San Francisco: Chandler.

Lane, R. E. (1959), *Political Life: How and Why Do People Get Involved in Politics?* New York: The Free Press.

Lyons, P., and R. Sinnott (2003), 'Voter Turnout in 2002 and Beyond', in M. Gallagher, M. Marsh and P. Mitchell (eds.), *How Ireland Voted 2002.* London: Palgrave Macmillan.

Murphy, G. (2003), 'The Background to the Election', in M. Gallagher, M. Marsh and P. Mitchell (eds.), *How Ireland Voted 2002.* London: Palgrave Macmillan.

Putnam, R. D. (2000), *Bowling Alone: The Collapse and Revival of American Community.* New York: Simon and Schuster.

Southwell, P. L. (1985), 'Alienation and Nonvoting in the United States: A Refined Operationalization', *Western Political Quarterly* 38: 663–74.

Appendix 5A *Correlations between the different components of political alienation: interest, trust, personal efficacy, system efficacy and knowledge.*

| | High levels of . . . | | | | |
|---|---|---|---|---|---|
| | Personal efficacy | System efficacy | Political trust | Political knowledge | Political interest |
| Personal efficacy | | | | | |
| System efficacy | .33 | | | | |
| Political trust | .10 | .27 | | | |
| Political knowledge | .38 | .19 | .16 | | |
| Political interest | .45 | .26 | .16 | .40 | |

**Note:** all pearson correlations statistically significant at .001 level (one tailed)

Appendix 5B *Effect of social characteristics on levels of political alienation: multi-variate ols regression (standardized coefficients).*

| | Higher levels of . . . | | | | |
|---|---|---|---|---|---|
| | Interest | Trust | Personal efficacy | System efficacy | Knowledge |
| Female | −.21+ | −.07‡ | −.23+ | −.12+ | .−23+ |
| Older | .24+ | .12+ | .17+ | .05* | .33+ |
| More educated | .17+ | −.01 | .21+ | .17+ | .21+ |
| Higher social class | .13+ | .04 | .20+ | .16+ | .12+ |
| Low religious attendance | −.06‡ | −.15+ | −.02 | .00 | .15+ |
| Urban | .03* | −.02 | .02 | .06* | 0.7+ |
| Adjusted r–square | .14 | .05 | .17 | .09 | .24 |

**Note**: scales used in this analysis and not categorical versions of the variables.
* statistically significant at .05 level
‡ statistically significant at .01 level
+ statistically significant at .001 level.

# 6. Irish Social and Political Cleavages

*Fiachra Kennedy and Richard Sinnott*[1]

In this chapter we outline the main political divisions ('cleavages') that exist across Europe and assess the extent to which the same patterns of division are observable in Ireland. We identify four traditional divisions operating in Irish politics: secular–liberals versus religious–conservatives; weak versus strong nationalists; egalitarians versus non-egalitarians; and free marketeers versus government interventionists. We also focus on two new divisions, which relate to EU integration and the environment. We use evidence from the Irish Social and Political Attitudes Survey (ISPAS) 2002 to identify where citizens stand on each of these themes. Then we assess whether different groups in society – men versus women, higher- versus lower-educated and so on – adopt different positions. Finally, the impact of these six social and political divisions on party preferences in Ireland is assessed. If these political divisions have any relevance to Irish people, they ought to influence, among other things, people's support for political parties.

## Types of Social and Political Cleavages

In their seminal analysis of political cleavages across Europe, Lipset and Rokkan (1967) focus on the following two sources of cleavages: the creation of the nation state and the industrial revolution. The first gives rise to the 'centre–periphery' cleavage and to the 'confessional–secular cleavage' and the second gives rise to the 'ownership of capital' cleavage.[2] We identify which of these generic types of political divisions is

1. The authors are grateful to Dr Fiona Gill and the editors for their considered comments and advice; any errors are our responsibility.
2. Lipset and Rokkan also identify a further cleavage, which has arisen from industrialization: the 'urban–rural' cleavage, which relates to the conflict between the interests of the emerging industrial economy and society, in particular the 'rising class of industrial entrepreneurs'; and those of the agrarian economy and society, 'the landed interests' (Lipset and Rokkan, 1967: 14). This is not considered here, since it is much less salient across contemporary Europe than the other cleavages identified.

most relevant in contemporary Ireland and whether there are new cleavages that have arisen in recent times.

## Cleavages around the National Revolution

The centre–periphery cleavage identified by Lipset and Rokkan relates to the conflict between centralized nation-building forces and citizens who live on the periphery, who are 'ethnically, linguistically, or religiously distinct subject populations' (1967: 14). This general pattern of division seems to have a direct relevance for Ireland. At the beginning of the twentieth century, Ireland (the periphery) managed to weaken and eventually break its links with Britain (the centre). Disappointments over delays in the introduction of Home Rule, the Easter Rising of 1916, the success of Sinn Féin in the election of 1918, and the War of Independence in the early 1920s all contributed to the emergence of 'radical nationalism'. Ireland's secession from Britain quickly resulted in a civil war between extreme and moderate nationalists, a war that served to intensify the centre–periphery (or nationalist) cleavage.

In the years following the civil war, the division within Irish nationalism contributed to the emergence of the two main political parties of the new state, Fianna Fáil and Fine Gael. Attitudes to the partition of the island remained polarized, with the more extreme nationalists desiring unification through the removal – by force if necessary – of the British presence in the north, while more moderate nationalists sought unification through consensus and a managed departure. The more extreme form of Irish nationalism was reinforced by events in the north, such as Bloody Sunday (1972) and the hunger strikes (1981), but the outbreak of political violence tempered the nationalism of many in the south. In 1998, the passing of the constitutional change to Article 2 marked a shift from a jurisdictional claim over territory ('the national territory . . . the whole island of Ireland, its islands and territorial seas') to the less hardline claim of a clear link between the territory of the whole island of Ireland and the Irish nation ('it is the entitlement and birthright of every person born in the island of Ireland . . . to be part of the Irish nation'). While the Good Friday Agreement attained massive support in the south, there are still differences of emphasis in the Republic of Ireland on the national issue – between those who seek to break the British connection with Ireland and those who work towards a consensus between the two traditions.

In addition to the Northern Ireland question, a potential new 'centre–periphery' cleavage is Ireland's relationship with the European Union. This relates to a division between those who favour a highly integrated EU and those who favour retaining as much sovereignty and independence as possible at the national level. A simple consideration of Ireland's geographical situation highlights Ireland's peripheral position as an 'island behind an island'. Whereas London was the 'old centre', Brussels and Frankfurt arguably form the 'new centre'. Over the last few decades, the Irish have been quite enthusiastic participants in the EU project, with, for the most part, positive attitudes towards the EU. The continued deepening of the process of integration and the introduction of the Euro have met with little resistance and have introduced new sources of identity for many. That said, there remains a proportion of the population who oppose further 'sharing of sovereignty' and are concerned about the impact Ireland's involvement in the EU is having on Irish identity, values and culture. Although Eurosceptics are a minority in Ireland, when turnout for referendums on EU treaties is low they form a large enough group to have a significant effect on the outcome (as happened in the Nice referendum in 2001). As further deepening of EU integration continues over the next few decades, and as the focus of attention of the 'centre' shifts towards the new member states from Central and Eastern Europe, it is likely that this version of the centre–periphery cleavage will become more salient.

According to Lipset and Rokkan, national revolutions give rise not only to centre–periphery cleavages but also to a confessional–secular cleavage. This is the division between the nation state that is seeking to centralize, standardize and mobilize, and the Church, which is seeking to protect its position of influence over what the emerging state considers to be its citizens (Lipset and Rokkan, 1967: 14). This church–state conflict may not have been very relevant in the early history of the Republic of Ireland, but has achieved high salience in recent decades.

When the Irish Free State was created, the vast majority of Irish people were Roman Catholic. The religious homogeneity of society, the high degree of religious practice and the close relationship between the Catholic Church and the nationalist movement ruled out the possibility of the development of a confessional–secular cleavage in Irish society for several decades. However, as Ireland became more open to ideas from the outside world, secularizing and liberalizing tendencies began to enter the scene. Highly divisive referendums on the issues of divorce (1986 and 1995) and abortion (1983, 1992 and 2002) revealed the potency of the divide between liberals, who resisted what they saw as the imposition of Catholic beliefs on society, and conservatives, who wished to defend the application of religious principles to the public realm. In recent years, the number of people who regularly attend church services has fallen and the Church's reputation has been badly undermined by a series of abuse scandals, leading to a waning of the influence of the Church in Irish society. This trend in Ireland is similar to that experienced in other European countries. However, the values the churches promote continue to influence many people. As Davie notes (1992: 223), while many Europeans may no longer practise religious faith, 'they have not abandoned, so far, many of their deep-seated religious motivations'

## Cleavages around the Industrial Revolution

Lipset and Rokkan identify the emergence, as a consequence of industrialization, of conflict over the 'ownership of capital'. Here, the division is between the 'owners and employers', on the one hand, and on the other, the 'tenants, labourers, and workers' (Lipset and Rokkan, 1967: 14). This is generally seen as the economic left–right divide that has characterized the contemporary politics of most European countries. The social democratic (or, formerly, socialist) left advocates a fairly coherent set of policy positions: a relatively strong role for trade unions to protect workers against exploitation by bosses; relatively high levels of progressive taxation by government, in order to redistribute wealth and foster economic equality; and high levels of government ownership of industry and services. The right generally offers opposing views, favouring limited trade-union powers, limited government interference via taxation and a strongly free-market approach to economic management.

It has long been felt that this economic left–right divide, which is the key cleavage in most European countries, has a much lower salience in Ireland, whose politics grew more out of the national struggle than the class struggle. When the Irish Free State was created, its economy was overwhelmingly agrarian. This, combined with the dominance of the Roman Catholic Church, meant that the prospects for the emergence of an owners versus workers – or economic left–right – cleavage were very weak. These prospects were further weakened when the Labour Party opted out of the 1918 election (an election that turned out to be the foundation election of the emerging political order of an independent Ireland) and by the poor levels of industrialization in Ireland. Agriculture continued to dominate the Irish economy for many decades, and while the industrial sector began to grow in the 1960s and for a time in the 1970s, the 1980s was a decade of economic depression.

Much of Ireland's recent economic growth is based not on the industrial sector but on the services sector. Ireland's economy is now, in significant part, a post-industrial economy that is reliant on a combination of inward investment, access to the European Union, and an educated, English-speaking workforce. Ireland's economic history appears to be that of a country passing from an agrarian economy to a post-industrial economy without really passing through the stage most associated with the emergence of a left–right cleavage, that of being an industrial economy. Thus, we are probably less likely to find a coherent set of 'left–right' views held by citizens. However, we will investigate two key issue areas commonly associated with the economic left–right divide – economic equality and the free market – and assess the extent to which they may or may not form a coherent single economic left–right dimension.

## The Environment as a Political Cleavage

Since the 1970s there has been much discussion about the emergence of new cleavages. Proponents of this view have argued that the cleavages around which political competition and conflict were once located are now being challenged by new issues. In particular, scholars have referred to the emergence of a materialist–postmaterialist dimension (MPM) (Inglehart, 1977, 1984, and 1990). The development of an MPM dimension is held to be a consequence of the conditions that prevailed in Western society after the Second World War, an era of economic prosperity, rising affluence and internal and international security (at least in terms of stable nuclear deterrence). The MPM dimension is associated with a set of 'new' issues such as quality of life, the environment, women's rights, and so on (Knutsen, 1990; Poguntke, 1987). However, the MPM dimension has been subjected to various criticisms, including the extent to which citizens hold postmaterialist values (Lijphart, 1981; van Deth, 1983; Clarke and Dutt, 1991; and Shively, 1991). Lijphart (1981: 40–41) argues that 'postmaterialism has so far not become the source of a new ideological dimension in many party systems'; and that in Inglehart's surveys of 1970, 1973 and 1976, 'the average proportion of postmaterialist respondents that he found was a meagre 11.5 per cent'.

While there is some question about the relevance of the MPM dimension, one issue associated with it – concern about the environment – has increased in salience in the minds of the general public in recent decades.[3] The importance of these concerns is reflected in the election of members of 'green' or 'ecological' political parties to national legislatures. In Ireland, the Green Party has experienced electoral success since the mid-1980s and in the most recent election in 2002 saw its number of parliamentary representatives increase from two to six. What remains to be established is whether support for the Green Party in Ireland is a consequence of the emergence of an environmental cleavage in Irish society.

---

3.  See also Motherway and Kelly (Chapter 2) and Kelly et al. (2003).

## Measuring the Six Social and Political Cleavages

We now use batteries of questions in the ISPAS 2002 Survey to operationalize and measure each of the six social and political divisions described above. In order to tap the nationalist cleavage, we draw on the responses to three questions asked in the ISPAS Survey that refer directly to Northern Ireland (see Table 6.1). Almost two-thirds of respondents favoured a united Ireland as a 'long-term policy'. Similarly, a clear majority – 62 per cent – agreed that 'there will never be a lasting peace in Northern Ireland until partition is ended'. However, these seemingly strongly nationalist responses are somewhat tempered in that only just over half wanted the British government to declare its intention to withdraw at a fixed date.

In relation to the European Union (see Table 6.2), while three-quarters of respondents stated that Ireland's membership has been a 'good thing', people are less convinced about further deepening: only one-third of respondents said they believed that 'unification has not gone far enough' and the same proportion agreed that Ireland should 'unite fully' with the EU. However, this is not to say that the Irish are against further integration, since only 17 per cent stated that integration has 'gone too far'. Instead, it would appear that a lot of Irish people are undecided about further integration.

In order to tap citizens' positions on the liberal–conservative (or 'secular–religious') dimension, we asked respondents how often they attend religious services, about their attitudes to the role of God in people's lives and whether or not abortion is ever justified. Three-quarters of respondents agreed that 'God should play a central role in

Table 6.1 *Attitudes to Irish unification (%)*

|  | Disagree | Neither agree/disagree | Agree |
|---|---|---|---|
| The long–term policy for Northern Ireland should be to reunify with the rest of Ireland | 16.2 | 19.4 | 64.4 |
| There will never be a lasting peace in Northern Ireland until partition is ended | 19.6 | 18.7 | 61.7 |
| The British government should declare its intention to withdraw from Northern Ireland at a fixed date in the future | 20.6 | 25.5 | 53.9 |

Table 6.2 *Attitudes to EU integration (%)*

|  | Euro-enthusiast response | Centrist response | Eurosceptic response |
|---|---|---|---|
| Ireland's membership of the EU | | | |
|     is a: good thing/bad thing | 75.3 | 19.9 | 4.8 |
| European unification has: not gone | | | |
|     far enough/already gone too far | 34.7 | 48.5 | 16.8 |
| Unite fully/protect independence | 34.9 | 36.5 | 28.6 |

**Note**: 0–10 scales were used as the response categories to these questions and these scales were summarized into three categories (0–3, 4–6, and 7–10).

Table 6.3 *Attitudes to economic management and redistribution (%)*

|  | Left Response | Centrist response | Right response |
|---|---|---|---|
| **Issues relating to redistribution** | | | |
| It is the government's responsibility | | | |
|     to reduce the differences in income | | | |
|     between people with high incomes | | | |
|     and those with low incomes | 65.4 | 14.7 | 19.9 |
| Government should redistribute income | | | |
|     from the better-off to those who are | | | |
|     less well off | 54.7 | 16.3 | 29.0 |
| The government should do all it can to | | | |
|     eliminate the gap between people with | | | |
|     high and low incomes | 59.6 | 7.1 | 33.3 |
| **Issues relating to the free market** | | | |
| Private enterprise is the best way | | | |
|     to solve Ireland's economic problems | 21.9 | 29.6 | 48.5 |
| Most of industry should be state- | | | |
|     owned and run/privately owned and run | 11.7 | 39.4 | 48.9 |
| The best way to provide services such as | | | |
|     hospitals, education and pensions is | | | |
|     through organizations set up and run by | | | |
|     the state/by involving private companies | | | |
|     and organizations | 23.9 | 44.1 | 32.0 |

people's lives' (12 per cent disagreed and the remainder 'neither agreed nor disagreed'). However, when it comes to attendance at religious services, 61 per cent of respondents said they attend at least once a week. Twenty-six per cent of respondents attend religious services a few times a year or less frequently. In relation to attitudes towards abortion, 51 per cent of the respondents believed it is never justified (i.e. on a 0 (never justified) to 10 (always justified) scale they placed themselves between 0 and 3). Perhaps not surprisingly, given the debates about this issue that took place between 2002 and 2004 one-third (34 per cent) of Irish respondents lie between the extremes (i.e. between 4 and 6 on the 10 point scale).

In terms of an economic left–right cleavage, two separate issue areas are explored, as noted: economic equality and government intervention in the economy. In terms of economic equality, most Irish respondents can be described as being on the left. Clear majorities – see Table 6.3 – agreed that it is 'the responsibility of the government to reduce income differences' (65 per cent); to redistribute income from the better-off to those who are less well off' (55 per cent); and to 'eliminate the gap' between rich and poor (60 per cent). However, when it comes to government intervention in the economy, Irish people are, on balance, more right-wing than left-wing. Almost half of respondents agreed that 'private enterprise is the best way to solve Ireland's economic problems', while only one-fifth disagreed. There is an even stronger trend in a right-wing direction on the question of ownership of industry. However, when it comes to providing services such as health and education, only one-third believed that private companies should be involved, while just less than a quarter believed that these services should be provided by state organizations.[4]

Table 6.4 *Attitudes to the environment (%)*

|  | Materialist | Centrist | Pro-Environment |
|---|---|---|---|
| There should be more economic growth and jobs, even if this means damage to the environment/we should protect the environment even if this means less economic growth and fewer jobs | 14.1 | 32.7 | 53.2 |
| I do what is right for the environment even when it costs more money or takes more time | 24.2 | 19.3 | 56.5 |
| Willing versus unwilling to pay much higher taxes in order to protect the environment | 51.6 | 14.3 | 34.1 |

4. A principal components factor analysis – reported in Appendix 6A – suggests that the equality and free-market dimensions should be treated separately rather than as a single, coherent, economic left–right dimension. The analysis suggests that there are indeed six distinct political cleavages/political dimensions, relating to: nation; EU; morality; equality; the free market; and the environment.

Finally, in relation to attitudes to the environment, our first question – see Table 6.4 – focused on the trade-off between care for the environment on the one hand and economic growth on the other. Just over 50 per cent of respondents prioritized the environment over growth and jobs. A slightly higher percentage claimed that they 'do what is right for the environment', even when it costs them more time or money. However, only slightly more than one-third of respondents stated that they were willing to pay 'much higher taxes in order to protect the environment', indicating that positive attitudes to caring for the environment are undermined once the subject of funding such care enters into the equation.

## Where Do the Different Social Groups Lie on Each of these Dimensions?

Do men and women hold different beliefs in relation to these political cleavages? Are higher-educated people different from less-educated people? What about the urban/rural and age distinctions? To make our comparisons between these groups as simple as possible, we created a single measure for each of our six cleavages.[5] (We did this by summing the responses of the set of items relating to each cleavage.) We then divided each of our six measures in two. We identified a proportion of respondents who were: relatively strong nationalists; relatively strong moral conservatives; relatively strong pro-Europeans; relatively strongly pro-equality; relatively strongly pro-government intervention in the market; and relatively strong environmentalists. (The cut-off point was 3.5 on a five-point scale.)

It emerges – see Table 6.5 – that men are more likely than women to be strongly nationalist. Older people, less-educated people and rural dwellers also tend to be relatively nationalist. Very strong effects emerge for the moral dimension, in that older people, less-educated people and rural people tend to be morally conservative. Also, men tend to be less conservative than women. Relatively strong pro-Europeans tend to be disproportionately male, young, educated and urban. Older people and those with less education are more likely to favour policies that are intended to redistribute wealth, but no strong demographic effects emerge for the government intervention cleavage. Finally, being highly educated emerges as the best predictor of holding relatively strong pro-environment views.

---

5.  Cronbach's alpha is an index of reliability of scales that ranges from 0 to 1. The higher the score on the index the more reliable is the scale. Whgile 0.7 is regarded as a threshold, less reliable scales are sometimes used in the literature. Of the scales we use, only two are close to this threshold: nationalism (0.73) and religious-moral (0.63). European integration (0.54), equality (0.53), government intervention (0.52) and environmentalism (0.41) fall some way short.

Table 6.5 *Percentage of socio-demographic cohorts that scored highly on each of the six value cleavages (greater than 3.5 on 1–5 scales).*

| | Strong Nationalism | Conservative Moral | Pro-Integration | Equality Left | Intervention Left | Pro-Environment |
|---|---|---|---|---|---|---|
| **TOTAL** | 51.6 | 67.2 | 53.2 | 49.9 | 11.7 | 37.8 |
| **Sex** | | | | | | |
| Male | 55.7 | 64.2 | 59.3 | 49.7 | 8.8 | 40.1 |
| Female | 48.3 | 69.6 | 48.3 | 50.1 | 14.2 | 35.9 |
| **Age** | | | | | | |
| 16–34 years | 46.9 | 47.0 | 56.8 | 40.3 | 13.9 | 30.3 |
| 35–54 years | 48.0 | 69.1 | 52.9 | 51.5 | 11.6 | 41.2 |
| 55+ years | 60.8 | 84.7 | 50.4 | 57.9 | 9.5 | 41.8 |
| **Education** | | | | | | |
| Junior Cert. | 58.9 | 76.0 | 46.2 | 58.8 | 15.9 | 30.9 |
| Leaving Cert. | 49.4 | 63.6 | 56.4 | 45.2 | 8.0 | 37.8 |
| Third Level | 42.1 | 57.4 | 61.1 | 41.9 | 9.4 | 47.5 |
| **Location** | | | | | | |
| Rural | 56.3 | 76.0 | 48.7 | 49.7 | 10.6 | 35.8 |
| Urban | 47.1 | 58.3 | 57.7 | 49.7 | 12.8 | 39.9 |

Lowest Ns: male = 525; female = 604; 18–34 years = 359; 35–54 years = 437;
55+ years = 328; junior certificate = 465; leaving certificate = 323; third level = 340; rural = 573; urban = 525.
Figures in bold indicate that the percentage for a given group is statistically significantly different from the total percentage at the .01 level or better.
*Source:* ISPAS 2002.

## Impact of Social and Political Cleavages on Party Preference

One way to examine the relevance of citizens' views on these social and political themes is to explore the relationship between their views and their support for the various political parties in Ireland. The measure of party support used in this chapter taps how likely it is that a respondent would ever give a first-preference vote to each of the main political parties. Respondents were asked to score each of the parties on a ten-point scale, where one meant that it was 'not at all probable' that they would ever give their first-preference vote to the party and ten meant that it was 'very probable' that they would do so. One of the advantages of this 'Probability to Vote' (PTV) question is that it captures a general attitude of each respondent towards *all* of the main political parties in Ireland (rather than simply asking respondents to indicate their most favoured party).

Appendix 6B reports the results of a multivariate analysis in which the unique impact of each political cleavage on party preference, controlling for the impact of other cleavages and social characteristics, is identified. It emerges – in line with conventional wisdom – that respondents with relatively nationalist views are more likely to vote for Fianna Fáil and Sinn Féin than those with less nationalistic views. On the issue of the EU, one would expect that, since the Green Party and Sinn Fein canvassed on the 'No' side of recent referendums on EU treaties, there would be a negative relationship between this value cleavage and support for these parties, and a positive relationship with support for the other parties. However, the EU attitudinal dimension does not have a significant impact on support for the Greens, Sinn Féin, Fianna Fáil, or Fine Gael. Positive attitudes to the EU are associated with support for Labour and the Progressive Democrats. With regard to the religious–moral scale, it is evident that those with more conservative values are more willing to support Fianna Fáil, while those with more liberal values support Labour, the Green Party and Sinn Féin.

What about those value cleavages associated with industrialization? It is difficult to state a priori whether or not these cleavages would have positive or negative effects on support for Fianna Fáil or Fine Gael, since both of these parties are fairly pragmatic in their approach to the economy. On the other hand, one would expect that these dimensions would have positive effects on the more socialist-leaning Labour Party, the Greens and on Sinn Féin, and a negative effect on the Progressive Democrats, who take a more conservative approach to the economy. On the economic equality scale, those who have left-leaning attitudes are more likely to vote for the more socialist parties, Labour and the Greens, than those with opposing attitudes; while those with right-leaning attitudes to government intervention in the economy are indeed more likely to favour the Progressive Democrats than those with more left-leaning attitudes.

Finally, in relation to the 'new' issue of the environment, one would expect that this cleavage would be the most important with regard to support for the Green Party. But what about the other political parties? One might argue that the other parties would favour economic growth over the environment, as each sought to protect a variety of economic interests. However, given the increased salience of environmental concern, at least in terms of acknowledging the importance of looking after the environment, a priori expectations about the relationship between this value cleavage and support for political parties is not quite so clearcut. In terms of support for the Green Party, the environmental value cleavage is by far the most important. It should also be noted, however, that this value cleavage also has an important positive impact on support for Fine Gael, Labour and the Progressive Democrats.

## Conclusion

Relying on a comparative framework, we have identified the social and political cleavages that divide Irish society. We conclude that Irish society is divided along six cleavage lines. The six relate to Northern Ireland, religious–moral matters, the European Union, equality, government intervention and the environment. Of these, two stand out as being of key importance: nationalism and the religious–moral dimension.

Nationalism had a crucial influence on the development of party politics in Ireland. In more recent years it has become a less salient issue in general elections and there is a general acceptance of the Good Friday Agreement's principle of consent. Nevertheless, a sizeable proportion of Irish people are still committed to a strong nationalist position.

For many decades Irish people were committed to the practice of their religious beliefs and the Roman Catholic Church had strong ties to the Irish state in terms of influence and the provision of 'public' services such as health and education. However, since the late 1960s, liberalizing and secular influences, as well as scandals in the 1990s, undermined the position of the church. That three-quarters of Irish people believe that God should play a role in their lives suggests that Irish people continue to cherish the spiritual. On the issue of abortion, which some see in religious or ideological terms, the evidence suggests that Irish society is divided into three approximately equal camps: conservatives, liberals and pragmatists.

The other cleavages would appear to be less important. There is still little evidence of the emergence of a single 'left–right' socio-economic cleavage in Ireland. Instead Irish society leans to the 'left' on economy. The environment dimension is the weakest of the six and contrary to expectations the materialist–postmaterialist scale was not strongly associated with this theme. One dimension that may become more salient in the decades to come is a new centre–periphery conflict over Ireland's relations with the European Union.

Overall, despite all of the changes in Ireland over the last decade or so, the two most important and durable cleavages in Irish society focus on nationalism and religion.

# References

Clarke, H. D., and N. Dutt (1991), 'Measuring Value Change in Western Industrialized Societies', *American Political Science Review* 85: 905–20.

Davie, G. (1992), 'God and Caesar: Religion in a Rapidly Changing Europe', in J. Bailey (ed.), *Social Europe*. London: Longman: 216–38.

Inglehart, R. (1977), *The Silent Revolution: Changing Values and Political Styles among Western Publics*. Princeton, NJ: Princeton University Press.

Inglehart, R. (1984), 'The Changing Structure of Political Cleavages in Western Society', in R. J. Dalton, S. C. Flanagan and P. A. Beck (eds.), *Electoral Change in Advanced Industrial Democracies: Realignment or Dealignment?* Princeton, NJ: Princeton University Press.

Inglehart, R. (1990), *Cultural Shift in Advanced Industrial Society*. Princeton, NJ: Princeton University Press.

Kelly, M., F. Kennedy, H. Tovey and P. Faughnan (2003), 'Cultural Sources of Support on Which Environmental Attitudes and Behaviours Draw'. Dublin: Environmental Protection Agencies.

Kim, J.-O., and C. W. Muller (1994a), 'Introduction to Factor Analysis: What it Does and How to Do it', in M. S. Lewis-Beck (ed.), *Factor Analysis and Related Techniques, International Handbooks of Quantitative Applications in the Social Sciences* 5. London: Sage.

Kim, J.-O., and C. W. Muller (1994b), 'Factor Analysis: Statistical Methods and Practical Issues', in M. S. Lewis-Beck (ed.), *Factor Analysis and Related Techniques, International Handbooks of Quantitative Applications in the Social Sciences* 5. London: Sage.

Knutsen, O. (1990), 'The Materialist–Post-Materialist Value Dimension as a Party Cleavage in the Nordic Countries', *West European Politics* 13: 258–74.

Lijphart, A. (1981), 'Political Parties: Ideologies and Programs', in D. Butler, H. Penniman and A. Ranney (eds.), *Democracy at the Polls: A Comparative Study of Competitive National Elections*. Washington, DC: American Enterprise Institute.

Lipset, S. M., and S. Rokkan (1967), 'Cleavage Structures, Party Systems and Voter Alignments: An Introduction', in S. M. Lipset and S. Rokkan (eds.), *Party Systems and Voter Alignments*. New York: Free Press.

Poguntke, T. (1987), 'New Politics and Party System: The Emergence of a New Type of Party'?, *West European Politics* 10: 76–88.

Shively, W. P. (1991), 'Cultural Shift in Advanced Industrial Society', *Journal of Theoretical Politics* 53.1: 235–38.

van Deth, J. W. (1983), 'The Persistence of Materialist and Post-Materialist Value Orientations', *European Journal of Political Research* 11: 63–79.

van Deth, J. W., and E. Scarbrough (1995), 'The Concept of Values', in J. W. van Deth and E. Scarbrough (eds.), *The Impact of Values: Beliefs in Government* 4: 21–47. Oxford: Oxford University Press.

Appendix 6A  *Final factor analysis of ISPAS social and political items*.*

|  | 1 | 2 | 3 | 4 | 5 | 6 |
|---|---|---|---|---|---|---|
| The long–term policy for Northern Ireland should be to reunify with the rest of Ireland[a] | 0.81 | | | | | |
| There will never be a lasting peace in Northern Ireland until partition is ended[a] | 0.80 | | | | | |
| The British government should declare its intention to withdraw from Northern Ireland at a fixed date in the future[a] | 0.79 | | | | | |
| How often nowadays do you attend religious services[b] (f24) | | 0.76 | | | | |
| God should play a central role in people's lives[a] (a3_3) | | 0.70 | | | | |
| Abortion: Never/always justified[b] (a4_2) | | 0.62 | | | | |
| Ireland should do all that it can to unite fully with the EU/to protect its independence from the EU[b] (a5_4) | | | 0.74 | | | |
| Ireland's membership of the EU is a bad/good thing[a] (a5_1) | | | 0.70 | | | |
| European unification has already gone too far/not gone far enough[a] (a5_8) | | | 0.69 | | | |
| It is the responsibility of the government to reduce the differences in income between people with high incomes and those with low incomes[b] (e1_2) | | | | 0.73 | | |

Appendix 6A *Continued.*

| | 1 | 2 | 3 | 4 | 5 | 6 |
|---|---|---|---|---|---|---|
| Government should redistribute income from the better-off to those who are less well off[b] (e23_1) | | | | 0.72 | | |
| The government should do all it can to eliminate the gap between people with high and low incomes[a] (a11_2) | | | | 0.66 | | |
| Private enterprise is the best way to solve Ireland's economic problems (e1_1) | | | | | 0.75 | |
| Most of industry should be state-owned and run/privately owned and run (a5_7) | | | | | 0.69 | |
| The best way to provide services such as hospitals, education and pensions is through organizations set up and run by the state/by involving private companies and organizations[b] (a5_3) | | | | | 0.69 | |
| Very willing/Very unwilling to pay much higher taxes in order to protect the environment[b] (e5_2) | | | | | | 0.75 |
| I do what is right for the environment, even when it costs more money or takes more time[b] (e6_2) | | | | | | 0.64 |
| There should be more economic growth and jobs even if this means damage to the environment/should protect the environment even it this means less economic growth and fewer jobs[a] (a5_5) | | | | | | 0.56 |
| **Materialist–postmaterialist index** | | | | | | |
| *Variance Explained* | 10.51 | 9.06 | 8.93 | 8.24 | 8.20 | 7.49 |
| Eigenvalues | 2.01 | 1.85 | 1.68 | 1.64 | 1.58 | 1.36 |

[a] Recoded so that values are 1–5

[b] Reversed and recoded so that values are 1–5

Principal Component Analysis: Varimax Rotation with Kaiser Normalization (Six Factors Extracted).

**Note**: only factor loadings greater than 0.5 are included in the table.

*Source:* ISPAS 2002.

Appendix 6B  *Effects of social and political cleavages on party preference (controlling for social characteristics).*

| | FF | FG | LAB | PD | GRN | SF |
|---|---|---|---|---|---|---|
| Northern Ireland (less nationalist to more nationalist) | 0.38** | -0.15 | -0.08 | -0.11 | -0.10 | 0.78*** |
| | (0.15) | (0.14) | (0.12) | (0.12) | (0.13) | (0.12) |
| Moral (liberal–secular to conservative–religious) | 0.64*** | -0.18 | -0.58*** | -0.01 | -0.40** | -0.41** |
| | (0.23) | (0.21) | (0.18) | (0.18) | (0.19) | (0.17) |
| EU (sceptical to pro-EU) | 0.25 | 0.07 | 0.52*** | 0.31** | -0.01 | -0.17 |
| | (0.18) | (0.16) | (0.14) | (0.14) | (0.15) | (0.13) |
| Economic equality (right to left) | -0.26 | -0.22 | 0.28* | -0.04 | 0.34** | 0.19 |
| | (0.18) | (0.16) | (0.14) | (0.14) | (0.15) | (0.13) |
| Government intervention (right to left) | 0.13 | -0.08 | -0.09 | -0.40*** | 0.11 | 0.14 |
| | (0.19) | (0.17) | (0.15) | (0.15) | (0.16) | (0.14) |
| Environment (economy to environment) | 0.10 | 0.44** | 0.32** | 0.41*** | 1.18*** | 0.08 |
| | (0.19) | (0.17) | (0.15) | (0.15) | (0.16) | (0.14) |
| Female | -0.18 | 0.10 | 0.58** | 0.51** | 0.63*** | -0.41** |
| | (0.28) | (0.26) | (0.23) | (0.22) | (0.23) | (0.21) |
| Age | -0.02* | 0.03*** | -0.00 | -0.00 | -0.00 | -0.03*** |
| | (0.01) | (0.01) | (0.01) | (0.01) | (0.00) | (0.01) |
| Level of education | -0.14** | 0.07 | 0.05 | 0.14*** | 0.12** | -0.07 |
| | (0.06) | (0.06) | (0.05) | (0.05) | (0.05) | (0.04) |
| Attend religious services at least once a week | 0.03 | 0.14 | 0.45 | 0.26 | -0.20 | 0.08 |
| | (0.36) | (0.34) | (0.30) | (0.29) | (0.31) | (0.27) |
| Urban | -0.52* | -0.30 | 0.58** | 0.29 | 0.63*** | 0.14 |
| | (0.28) | (0.26) | (0.23) | (0.22) | (0.23) | (0.21) |
| Constant | 4.02** | 3.63 | 1.50 | 1.18 | -0.80 | 3.49*** |
| | (1.59) | (1.47) | (1.29) | (1.26) | (1.33) | (1.19) |
| Adj. $R^2$ | 0.05*** | 0.03*** | 0.08*** | 0.06*** | 0.15*** | 0.12*** |
| F–Ratio | 3.73 | 2.60 | 5.82 | 4.74 | 11.30 | 8.55 |
| N | 644 | 636 | 632 | 627 | 629 | 635 |

* significant at the 10 per cent level of significance; ** significant at the 5 per cent level of significance; *** significant at the 1 per cent level of significance

*Source:* ISPAS 2002.

# 7. Stability and Change in the Structure of Electoral Competition, 1989–2002

## *Michael Marsh*

Elections, almost by definition, are seen as occasions in which political parties compete for votes. In reality, that competition may be limited. It could be that many voters are effectively 'out of competition', having made a standing decision to support a particular party, which allows no effective consideration of any other party (see Mair, 1987: 63–64). For example, a voter may be extremely committed to Fianna Fáil and would never dream of giving a first-preference vote to any other party. In this case, all Fianna Fáil has to worry about is making sure that this voter turns out to vote on election day. Other voters may be genuinely trying to make up their minds about which of a number of parties to vote for. If a voter is only considering the merits of two parties in particular – Fine Gael and Labour, say – that voter is 'open to competition' between those two parties (and 'out of competition' for all the other parties). Other voters may be seriously considering voting for one or other of three or more parties and are thus open to competition between a range of parties. The existence of voters who are open to competition allows parties to compete with one another for votes (and not simply compete over which party can mobilize the largest proportion of its voters).

The traditional picture of the Irish electorate was one in which a large number of voters were removed from competition between parties. Instead, voters followed loyalties established during and after the civil war. Thus, you were either a Fianna Fáiler or a Fine Gaeler and a Fianna Fáiler would never seriously consider voting Fine Gael, while a Fine Gaeler would never seriously consider voting Fianna Fáil. The more common view nowadays is of an *available* electorate, one prone to violent swings towards or away from particular parties; an electorate cut off from its traditional moorings and free to float on whatever political tide is flowing. In short, many commentators believe that we now have an electorate that is open to competition between a range of parties – that we have, in fact, a large number of floating voters.

Certainly, we have seen some striking changes in Irish party politics over the last twenty-five years. At various times, the electorate has moved clearly towards or away from particular parties: towards Fine Gael in the early 1980s and away from that party in 1987 and 2002; towards Labour in 1992 and away from it in 1997; towards the Progressive Democrats in 1987 and away again in 1989; and towards the smaller opposition parties (Greens and Sinn Féin) in 2002. While these changes could be due to the extreme volatility of a small section of the electorate, they may also signify an electorate that is relatively unattached and so open to offers at each election – although not easily persuaded twice, perhaps. This volatility has been encouraged by changes in the traditional options for government. Fianna Fáil became open to coalition in 1989 when Charles Haughey and Des O'Malley formed the first Fianna Fáil–Progressive Democrats government; Fianna Fáil went on to govern with Labour and then again with the Progressive Democrats. Fine Gael governed with Labour in 1994–7, in a government that also included the Democratic Left. Labour has thus governed in two quite separate constellations since 1992 and, of course, kept both options open in the 2002 campaign. The Green Party is now also seen to be 'coalitionable', although circumstances have not yet favoured its entry into government, and even Sinn Féin can be spoken of as a potential partner for Fianna Fáil. Thus, a certain degree of promiscuity characterizes the relationships between Irish parties, which might lead us to expect wider competition and, in the absence of firm, long-term alliances (and no alliances), a lack of structure in that competition.

At the same time, however, there are also some signs of a greater distinctiveness in the options given to voters, at least with respect to the smaller parties. Judged in terms of their support base, the Green Party, the Progressive Democrats and Sinn Féin appear to be far from 'catchall' parties (as was the Worker's Party/Democratic Left before it merged with the Labour Party). Each is quite distinctive in terms of its social support and, to a lesser degree, the sorts of issues it appears to prioritize (Garry et al., 2003). It remains to be seen what impact this has on competition. The existence of such parties could close off competition by providing an 'ideal home' for certain sections of voters, and several such 'niche' parties might give more shape to electoral competition. The Progressive Democrats and Sinn Féin may provide a right and left pole for a party system that has long been seen as concentrated at the centre of the political spectrum. If so, these parties could help provide a structure to a competition that might otherwise appear amorphous.

Against this background, this chapter draws on data from the ISPAS 2002 Survey to explore the changing political inclinations of the Irish electorate and to establish some parameters for electoral competition. Using a battery of questions pioneered in the Netherlands (van der Eijk and Niemoller, 1983), which have now been employed extensively in electoral research in some other countries (van der Eijk and Oppenhuis, 1991; Oppenhuis, 1995; van der Eijk and Franklin, 1996), this chapter seeks to establish the extent to which the electorate is open to a real competition for votes between parties and the extent to which this competition is structured in predictable ways. With the aid of comparable data from a post-election survey carried out in 1989, it also explores the extent to which the degree and structure of competition has changed over the thirteen years between the two surveys.

## Measuring Competition

Questions that are asked in surveys about party preference typically focus on the outcome of the choice voters make – Did you (or, Will you) vote for party A, B or C? – and ignore the other options that voters may consider (How likely is it that you would vote for A? How likely is it that you would vote for B? How likely is it that you would vote for C?) Typically, surveys ask respondents who they would vote for if an election were to be held tomorrow (or who they voted for in the last election). What surveys do not ask is whether the party indicated by the respondent is the respondent's very *clear-cut* choice or whether the party is indicated after the respondent genuinely tries to decide between a *number* of parties. Yet this unasked question is important. Unless we have some way of finding the answer to it, we cannot establish the likelihood that things might change, or might have been different. The questions used here ask respondents to indicate for each party how likely it is – on a scale of 1–10 – that a given party would ever get their vote. The end points of the scale are labelled as follows: 1 means that a respondent would never vote for that party and 10 means that the respondent would certainly vote for that party.[1] The use of the word 'ever' here is intended

---

1. 'We have a number of political parties in Ireland, each of which would like to get your [first-preference] vote. How probable is it that you will ever give your first-preference vote to the following parties? Please use the number on this scale to indicate your views, where '1' means 'not at all probable' and '10' means 'very probable'. *[Interviewer shows card giving names of each of the parties, with a row of 10 boxes against each, and, according to the response, ticks one box on each line.]* In the Irish context there is, of course, a potential confusion about what is meant by 'vote': is it a first preference, or any lower preference? Some of these may be effectively indicating an extreme dislike of the party. However, the ISPAS Survey explored differences between the specific term 'first-preference vote' and the more general 'vote'. Each form of the question was asked of half of the respondents. A comparison of the two halves shows no statistically significant differences between the two sets of results, which implies that this aspect of the wording has no impact on the responses. The 1989 question used a different preamble, but is substantially the same: 'Some people always vote for the same party. Other people make up their mind each time. Please tell me for each of the following how probable it is that you will ever vote for this party in a general election.'

to get people to think in a somewhat more general way about a party, and provide a context wider than the immediate one. These questions measure the utility that each individual voter would derive from voting for each party and we thus refer to them as 'party utilities' (Tillie, 1995).

## Change and Stability in the Degree of Competition

This party utilities question is now used to examine the voter's orientation towards the various parties competing at any particular time. In 2002 we asked about Fianna Fáil, Fine Gael, Labour, Greens, Progressive Democrats, Sinn Féin and 'independents', although this last category is obviously a poorly defined one, since independent candidates vary a lot. The first thing to find out is how voters rate parties. This is shown in Table 7.1, which also gives comparable data for 1989.[2] In 2002, 78 per cent gave a high score to at least one party, a high score being 8, 9 or 10. Thirteen per cent gave a medium score (6 or 7) and 9 per cent a pretty low score (below 6). We might expect that for voters giving a low score, the main area of competition is between choosing whether or not to vote at all, rather than choosing between competing parties.[3] As Table 7.1 shows, since 1989 there has been a 7 per cent decline in the percentage of respondents giving a high score, something that might be expected given the significant drop in turnout over the period.

Table 7.1 *Distribution of scores for most favoured party, 1989 and 2002*

| | Score of Most Favoured Party (%) | | | |
|---|---|---|---|---|
| | High (8–10) | Medium (6–7) | Low (1–5) | Number of cases |
| 2002 | 78 | 13 | 9 | 2342 |
| 1989 | 85 | 10 | 5 | 954 |

Sources: 2002 ISPAS Survey, weighted to provide representative social background and 1997 vote; 1989 European election study, weighted by social background and 1989 national election vote. Missing data and respondents who gave all parties 1 are excluded.

2.  See van der Eijk and Oppenhuis (1991) for some comparative data on other EU countries.
3.  Those with low scores for their most favoured party or parties are much less likely to report having voted in 1997 or to be able to indicate any preference for a forthcoming general election.

The next aspect to explore is the number of parties that receive the highest score a respondent gives. To what extent do voters see one party as better than the rest (however poorly they rate that party); and to what extent do voters see several parties as equal? Table 7.2 shows the figures, again for 2002 and 1989. Sixty-nine per cent gave one party a lead over the rest in 2002, with the other 31 per cent putting two, three, four or more parties in first place. The distributions were almost identical in 1989. (I have excluded from subsequent analysis the 4 per cent of the sample who gave a '1' to each of the seven parties, treating them essentially as non-respondents, but left in those who rated all parties equally but did so with a score in excess of 1.)

Table 7.2  *Number of parties given best score, 1989 and 2001*

|  | *Number of Parties with Highest Scores (%)* | | | | | | | |
|---|---|---|---|---|---|---|---|---|
|  | *1* | *2* | *3* | *4* | *5* | *6* | *7* | *Number of cases* |
| 2002 | 69 | 16 | 7 | 2 | 1 | 1 | 4 | 2342 |
| 1989 | 68 | 18 | 7 | 3 | 2 | 1 | 2 | 954 |

*Sources:* 2002 ISPAS Survey, weighted to provide representative social background and 1997 vote; 1989 European election study, weighted by social background and 1989 national election vote.

I now examine the relationship between how voters rate their 'best' party and how many parties they rate together in first position. Do those voters who show a clear preference for one party always rate that party highly? Do those who seem to be undecided between several parties give them a low score? This is shown in Table 7.3, which again gives comparable figures for 1989. Most voters who have a clearly favoured party score that party highly. The 69 per cent of respondents in 2002 whose highest score was for a single party break down as follows: 64 per cent give that party a high score (between 8 and 10) and only five give it a relatively low score (between 1 and 7). By contrast, the 31 per cent whose highest score was for more than one party break down as follows: the highest score of 23 per cent is 'high' and the highest score of 8 per cent is 'not high'.

So, among those who tie two or more parties in first place, almost three-quarters also score these parties highly (although those with ties are much less likely to score their best parties highly than are those who have a clearly favoured party). Even so, among the 23 per cent who are very likely to vote for one of two or more parties, but cannot discriminate between them at present, there is considerable room for real competition. Once again, the figures for 1989 are very similar, although 'tied' favoured parties were more likely to be scored highly in 1989.

Table 7.3 *Distribution of scores for best party and numbers given best score, 1989 and 2002 (cell entries are percentages of sample)*

| Highest score for: | 2002 | | 1989 | |
|---|---|---|---|---|
| | *High (8–10)* | *Not High (1–7)* | *High (8–10)* | *Not High (1–7)* |
| One party | 64 | 5 | 64 | 4 |
| More than one party | 23 | 8 | 27 | 5 |

*Source:* 2002 ISPAS Survey, weighted to provide representative social background and 1997 vote; 1989 European election study, weighted by social background and 1989 national election vote. Missing data and respondents who gave all parties 1 are excluded.

These 'tied' voters, particularly those giving two or more parties a high score, correspond most obviously to the popular notion of floating voters, but do not by any means constitute all the voters to whom the 'floating voter' label might reasonably be applied. There are also those voters for whom the gap between best and next-best party is very small, say one or two points. Putting these two groups together, we see that 44 per cent rate at least one party highly and rate at least one other party as either equal or not more than two points behind. These voters are clearly 'in competition'. They may be contrasted with the 43 per cent who seem out of competition, having a clear preference for a particular party, which they rate highly ('clear' in the sense that the next most preferred party is more than two points away). The remainder – 13 per cent – have no strong preferences at all.

This distribution of these three types of voters – those 'in competition' (or floating voters), those out of competition and a residual group of apathetic or alienated voters – is somewhat changed from 1989. The size of the out-of-competition group is almost the same (42 per cent in 1989, as opposed to 43 per cent in 2002), but the group in competition was 53 per cent in 1989. One reason for the decline – evident in Table 7.3 – is that in 2002 fewer voters without a single top party rate their joint top parties in the 8–10 range. Another reason is that fewer of those with a clear top party rated their second party as being within one or two points of it. What this suggests is that there is actually a slightly smaller group of voters in competition now and more who are apathetic or alienated.

## Who Competes for the Floating Voters?

Having established that a high proportion of voters are in competition, or floating voters, I now want to see which particular parties they appear to be floating between. Floating voters are not necessarily those who may finish up anywhere. As we have seen, many have two, three or more parties for whom they are likely to vote. Another way to put this is to say that floating voters form part of the potential support for more than one party. (It is a 'potential' support because it is not the same as actual votes.) Using the concept of potential support, we can ask of each party: how much of its support does it share and with whom does it share it?

It could be that some parties are more insulated from the chilly wind of competition than others. In other words, a party may have lots of voters who score it very highly and do not score the other parties highly at all. In contrast, another party may have voters who score that party highly but also score other parties equally, or nearly equally. To start with, we need a measure of each party's potential support. One measure is to take the proportion of the electorate who rate that party most highly.[4] This has the advantage of simplicity, but it ignores the small differences that might exist between parties in any voter's mind. A more nuanced measure would use the full range of information given by the utility scores – and that is the one employed here. Following van der Eijk and Franklin (1996), I construct this by transforming the utility scores into a 0–1 scale and treating the transformed scores as probabilities. Remember that the lowest point (1) on the scale was labelled 'would never vote for this party'. Hence, a probability of a 0 is justified, as is a 1 for the tenth point on the scale ('would certainly vote for this party'). The remaining scores are mapped evenly on to the space between 0 and 1 (i.e. .11, .22, etc.). The average of these scores can be seen as a measure of that party's potential support in the electorate. Obviously low scores contribute very little. It takes nine voters with a score of 2 (transformed to 0.11) to make one potential supporter, so the bulk of potential support comes from respondents giving a party a high score.

The next step is to examine how one party's potential support overlaps with the potential support of another party. This can be calculated by contrasting the sum of the potential support for each party with the potential support for a combination of the two. This latter is obtained from each voter's score for the most highly rated of the two parties. If the

4. Analysis using this measure shows much less overlap between the support for different parties than is shown in Tables 7.4 and 7.5, but the pattern of overlap is similar, with sharing spread across the spectrum and Fianna Fáil supporters less inclined to share than the supporters of any other party.

same voters rate each party equally, the support for the two parties will overlap completely; if support comes from an entirely different set of voters, there will be no overlap. We have already seen that there is substantial evidence of overlapping support. Our analysis will tell us where overlapping occurs and how big it is. In this manner we may find out how potential support for Fine Gael, for instance, overlaps with that for Fianna Fáil and for the Progressive Democrats, for the Greens and for Labour. Thus:

> Proportion of support of party A shared with party B = (potential support for party A + potential support for party B – potential support for AB) divided by potential support for A.

However, we would also like to know how far each of this overlapping is due to the same voters and how far it comprises different sets of voters. In other words, does a party share all of its support with other parties, or is there some unique source of support that is effectively out of competition and belongs to that party alone. We can calculate this for a party by comparing the potential vote for all parties combined with the potential support for all parties except that one:

> Proportion of potential support of party A that is unique to party A = potential support for all parties (A, B, C and so on) minus potential support for all parties except A.

Figure 7.1 may help to explain the nature of overlaps and, in particular, how these may be asymmetrical. It shows the degree of overlap between

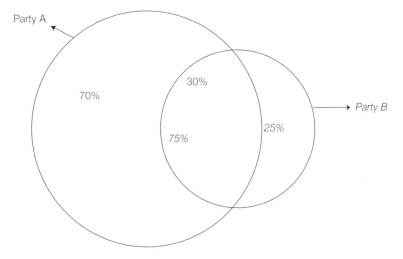

Figure 7.1 *Example of high party B/party A and low party A/party B overlap.*

the large potential support of party A and the smaller potential support for B. A shares 30 per cent of its support with B; 70 per cent is not shared but is unique to A. Party B, on the other hand, shares 75 per cent of its vote with party A and has only 25 per cent unique to itself.

Table 7.4 shows for each party its potential support, the extent to which each other party has a share of that support, and the extent to which it has a unique support shared with no other party. The table is most easily read downwards. For example, the potential support for Sinn Féin is 21 per cent. The support that belongs to Sinn Féin uniquely is 5 per cent. The overlap between the Sinn Féin potential support and that for the Green Party is 68 per cent, for Labour is 67 per cent, and so on. The table can also be read across, in which case it shows, for example, Sinn Féin's share of each party's potential support.

Table 7.4  *Overlap of each party's potential support, 2002*

|  | Potential Electorate of (%): | | | | | | |
|  | *SF* | *Green* | *Labour* | *IND* | *Fine Gael* | *PD* | *FF* |
|---|---|---|---|---|---|---|---|
| Potential support | 21 | 37 | 38 | 46 | 43 | 32 | 52 |
| % of support that is unique | 5 | 2 | 4 | 6 | 9 | 1 | 20 |
| *Shared with:* | | | | | | | |
| SF | 100 | 39 | 38 | 57 | 30 | 39 | 29 |
| Green | 68 | 100 | 71 | 61 | 60 | 69 | 47 |
| Labour | 67 | 72 | 100 | 60 | 62 | 73 | 47 |
| IND | 80 | 76 | 73 | 100 | 65 | 76 | 57 |
| Fine Gael | 61 | 69 | 69 | 61 | 100 | 74 | 54 |
| PDs | 58 | 66 | 62 | 53 | 55 | 100 | 48 |
| FF | 70 | 59 | 64 | 64 | 65 | 77 | 100 |

*Source:* 2002 ISPAS Survey, weighted to provide representative social background and 1997 vote.

The most obvious point to make about the 'potential support' figures is that they sum to much more than 100, indicating that there is a substantial overlap in the support for different parties. Remarkably, however, support levels are far more similar than we might expect. Most parties fail to translate most of their potential support into first preferences at the polls. Fianna Fáil and Fine Gael do best. Each of those parties has more unique support than other parties, but even in the case of Fianna Fáil, this amounts to only 20 per cent – one-fifth – of its potential support, giving it a base of just over 10 per cent [52 * 0.20] of the electorate.[5] At the other extreme, the Progressive Democrats share 99 per cent of their support with at least one other party. All this confirms the fact that parties share supporters, but who shares with whom? The rest of the table gives us the answer: each party shares with all the others.

Thus, Sinn Féin's largest percentage (80 per cent) is shared with independents and its smallest (58 per cent) with the Progressive Democrats and Fine Gael (61 per cent). What is most striking here is perhaps the degree of overlap. Fianna Fáil has the largest potential vote and the largest vote that is unique to the party. Not surprisingly, then, it also seems to share its voters with other parties much less than is typical elsewhere. But even so, it shares 54 per cent of its support with Fine Gael and 57 per cent with independents, sharing least with Sinn Féin (29 per cent). In addition to the degree of overlap, the general pattern of the overlapping support is also remarkable. The differences between the percentages are quite small, whether we read down the columns or across the rows. Hence, the share of the Fine Gael vote taken by each of the other parties varies only from 55 per cent to 65 per cent if we exclude Sinn Féin's 30 per cent share; and Fine Gael's share of each of the other parties' votes ranges from 54 per cent of Fianna Fáil's to 74 per cent of the Progressive Democrats' vote.

Looking back to 1989, there has been remarkably little change in the degree of overlap between the parties and thus in the general openness of the electorate. There are, of course, changes in the party system. In 1989, Fine Gael was stronger, Sinn Féin had no parliamentary representatives and the Green Party had just one, while the Workers' Party was a significant force with several TDs. No question was asked with respect to independents in 1989 (or the Workers' Party in 2002), so comparisons are limited. Table 7.5 shows the differences between 2002 and 1989. Positive numbers indicate an increase in 2002, negative numbers indicate a decrease.

Potential support for each of the parties has changed somewhat since 1989, most obviously for Fine Gael (down 5 per cent, a change that roughly matches Fine Gael's fate in the polls over that period) and Sinn Féin (up 8 per cent). Fianna Fáil's potential support is little changed, but that party would appear to have to compete more for the votes it gets, since the uniqueness of its support is less pronounced. In fact, no party increased its proportion of 'unique' support. In the main body of Table 7.5, where overlaps between pairs of parties are shown, the numbers are generally small: almost all change is smaller than 15 percentage

---

5. In assessing these potential votes, it should be borne in mind that the average of the highest transformed scores is less than $1 - 0.86$ in 2002 and 0.89 in 1989. This is because some voters give no score over 0, and substantial numbers do not give a maximum score to their most preferred party.

Table 7.5 *Changes in the overlap of each party's potential support between 2002 and 1989 (%)*

|  | SF | Green | Labour | Fine Gael | PD | FF |
|---|---|---|---|---|---|---|
| Potential support | +8 | −4 | +2 | −5 | −2 | −1 |
| Unique share of potential support | 0 | −2 | −1 | −2 | −2 | −5 |
| *Shared with:* | | | | | | |
| SF | – | +9 | +13 | +14 | +17 | 13 |
| Green | −25 | – | +4 | +5 | +5 | −2 |
| Labour | −9 | +6 | – | +10 | +11 | +4 |
| Fine Gael | 0 | +3 | +5 | – | −12 | −2 |
| PDs | −1 | +5 | +8 | −5 | – | +5 |
| FF | +5 | +3 | +8 | +4 | +11 | – |

*Source:* 2002 ISPAS Survey, weighted to provide representative social background and 1997 vote; 1989 European election study, weighted to provide representative social background and 1989 National election vote.

points and 16 of the 30 entries are 5 percentage points or less. The biggest changes largely relate to Sinn Féin. Its potential electorate was smaller in 1989 and consequently it took a smaller share of the potential vote of all the other parties. The other major changes since 1989 are the increased Labour share of the Fine Gael vote, a smaller Fine Gael share of the Progressive Democrats vote and a very significant drop in the Green share of the Sinn Féin vote. There is some sign of increased overlap between all parties, but the main pattern is one of stability in terms of the potential support for each of the parties and in the degree to which the support for each of the parties overlaps with that of other parties.

## Stability and Change in the Structure of Competition

In this section, I look at the overall structure of overlapping preferences to see to what extent they can be said to form a pattern. One way to do this is by examining Table 7.4 to see how far there seems to be some order evident in the way overlaps increase down the columns. In this table, the parties are presented in the left–right and top–bottom order that appears to best display a pattern of overlaps peaking once at the cell on the main diagonal (where the entry is 100 per cent). If there is an order, we should see the highest degrees of overlap between adjacent parties and the least between parties furthest away from one another. So we should see a big overlap between Fine Gael and the Progressive

Democrats, and a small one between Sinn Féin and the Progressive Democrats. By this criterion we might conclude that there is some sign of a pattern, but that it is not very strong. Even if we leave aside the independents, on the grounds that they do not constitute a coherent category, there are anomalies. Looking down the columns in Table 7.4, Fianna Fáil's share of Sinn Féin support is too high and the Progressive Democrats' share of the Fine Gael vote is too low. As we have seen before, the gradient – the degree of increase or decrease – is also very small. This suggests that while there may be a structure, it is not a very strong one. What the information in Table 7.4 does not tell us is how strong the structure is and whether some other ordering of the parties might result in a more strongly structured party system.

A more systematic way to analyse the underlying structure, and one that will enable us to make comparisons with 1989, is by the use of unfolding methods (Coombs, 1964). These methods attempt to construct a single spatial representation of persons and stimuli – in our case, voters and parties. The positions of voters and parties in this so-called joint space should be such that the distances between voters and parties reflect (inversely) the preferences that are observed empirically. In other words, the higher a voter's preference for a party, the smaller the distance between them in the spatial representation (in more formal terms this is known as 'the assumption of single-peaked preferences'). These relations should hold to a satisfactory degree for all persons and for all parties. If such a space can be constructed, the positions of voters and parties on the dimensions that define the space can be calculated and used to characterize them in further analyses. (These positions can also be used in the substantive interpretation of the dimensions, which is usually done by taking into account other known characteristics of the stimuli and of the subjects. I do not have enough space to do this here, but will deal with it in a later paper.)

These dimensions can be thought of as being cognitive in character (they indicate where voters perceive candidates, as well as themselves), and evaluative (distance on these dimensions determines, in an inverse way, the level of preference). An interesting aspect of such representations is that if they can be constructed, they indicate that *all* voters involved evaluate all parties to a large degree on the basis *of the same criteria*. Inability to construct such a spatial representation of the observed preferences can indicate several things. It may signify that not all parties are evaluated on the same criteria; it may signify that voters do not have (to a sufficient degree) the same perceptions of parties, or it may mean that not all preferences given by individual voters are based on the same criteria.

The number of parties is rather small for unfolding analysis. Therefore, it only makes sense to investigate the extent to which preferences for these parties can be represented in one-dimensional spaces.[6] Various algorithms for one-dimensional unfolding exist, all of which are designed for specific types of data. In this chapter we will use the unfolding algorithm MUDFOLD (van Schuur, 1984, 1988). The advantage of MUDFOLD over other available programmes is that it provides a goodness-of-fit measure – the H-coefficient – that can be used to compare the strength of a common dimension over time. It also allows us to compare the strength of scales containing different sets of stimuli. H attains an upper limit of 1 if the constructed scale represents the data perfectly, without any violations. If, on the other hand, a proposed scale yields as many violations with empirical observations as would occur in the case of statistical independence of the stimuli, H is 0. As a rule of thumb, H should be at least .30 if we are to treat a scale as meaningful, and above .50 if we are to see it as strong (Oppenhuis, 1995).

Figure 7.2 shows the results obtained with unfolding analysis using the sets of party scores already discussed. It shows the results for different sets of stimuli and displays an ordering in each case. (There is no significance to the area of space between each stimulus – party or independent group). We began by trying to find a scale on which all parties could be placed. The H coefficient for this full analysis (Figure 7.2a) is .40. That is above the minimal level of .30 but well below the typical level for other European party systems of around .50. The three parties on the left of the scale – Sinn Féin, Green and Labour – fit better into this structure than do the three on the right-hand side, and the independents fit worst of all. However, no alternative scale, such as is obtained by reversing Greens and Labour, gives quite such a good fit, and many obvious options, such as placing the Progressive Democrats to the right of Fianna Fáil, resulted in a much worse fit.

Arguably, independents are an inappropriate group for inclusion in this exercise because they are so disparate. Any particular independent might fit quite well, but a group that included Tony Gregory, Jackie Healy-Rae and Thomas Gildea may not have fitted easily into any framework. It could be that the attempt to treat this group as a single stimulus is the reason why the overall fit is not better. We tested this by running the analysis again, but this time without the independent stimulus, using only the set of six *party* stimuli. The ordering is the same, but the fit is improved, rising to .43 (Figure 7.2b). The structure owes much to the fact that Sinn Féin, the Greens and Labour are placed on one side and Fine Gael, Fianna Fáil and the Progressive Democrats on the other,

6. Multi-dimensional spatial representations would pose so few restrictions on the data that very different configurations would all fit the data perfectly, which implies that they would be trivial. Unidimensional representations of three or more stimuli will not by necessity fit well, so that if they do fit, a relevant empirical result has been attained.

Figure 7.2 *Unfolded scale orderings from potential electorates with goodness-of-fit coefficients for each party, 2002*

### (a) Including all parties and independents

| SF | Green | Labour | Indep. | FG | PD | FF |
|----|-------|--------|--------|----|----|----|
| .43 | .43 | .43 | .34 | .37 | .40 | .38 |

Overall goodness of fit: H = .40

### (b) Including parties only

| SF | Green | Labour | FG | PD | FF |
|----|-------|--------|----|----|----|
| .43 | .46 | .48 | .41 | .43 | .40 |

Overall goodness of fit: H = .43

**Note**: Data consists of the probability to vote questions from ISPAS. Analysis is carried out using MUDFOLD. Respondents rating all parties 1 are excluded.

but all parties fit satisfactorily into this pattern and moving any party worsens the overall fit.

How does this pattern compare with that for 1989? Is it stronger or weaker, and has the ordering of the parties changed over these thirteen years? In 1989, respondents were asked about the Workers' Party rather than about independents. We first examined the fit that could be obtained by putting the Workers' Party – a self-proclaimed left-wing party – between the Greens and Sinn Féin. As shown in Figure 7.3a, this gives a scale with a satisfactory H coefficient (.51) but it is evident that the Green Party fits less easily into this model than does any other party. In addition, we are not comparing like with like, because we would expect the Workers' Party to have provided a much more cohesive stimulus than the independents. We therefore examined the structure without the Worker's Party. This is Figure 7.3b.

Here, the fact that the Greens are a relatively poor fit is even more obvious. If we leave out the Greens (in Figure 7.3c), the resulting structure, which has a scale value of .51, is clearer. On this basis we might say that a change between 1989 and 2002 is that the Greens came to be seen by the electorate as close to Labour, whereas before, the electorate was more uncertain. However, this might understate the extent of change, since the best ordering in 1989 may be altogether different from that in 2002. In fact, an equally strong ordering is shown in Figure 7.3d. The most significant feature is that the positions of Fine Gael and the Progressive Democrats are reversed. The scale value is still .51, again much better than anything achievable in 2002.

Figure 7.3 *Unfolded scale orderings from potential electorates with goodness-of-fit coefficients for each party, 1989*

### (a) All parties

| SF | WP | Green | Labour. | FG | PD | FF |
|----|----|-------|---------|----|----|----|
| .71 | .61 | .38 | .53 | .52 | .51 | .45 |

Overall goodness of fit: H = .51

### (b) All parties except WP

| SF | Green | Labour | FG | PD | FF |
|----|-------|--------|----|----|----|
| .66 | .34 | .44 | .47 | .47 | .42 |

Overall goodness of fit: H = .45

### (c) All parties except WP and Greens

| SF | Labour | FG | PD | FF |
|----|--------|----|----|----|
| .61 | .48 | .52 | .53 | .47 |

A] Overall goodness of fit: H = .51

### A] (d) All parties except WP and Greens: FG, PD reversed

| SF | Labour | PD | FG | FF |
|----|--------|----|----|----|
| .61 | .48 | .52 | .53 | .47 |

Overall goodness of fit: H = .51

**Note**: Data consists of the probability to vote questions from ISPAS. Analysis is carried out using MUDFOLD. Respondents who rated all parties 1 are excluded.

This suggests that parties did move a little with respect to one another in the public mind between 1989 and 2002. In 1989, the Green Party's appeal was more amorphous; as a new party, it perhaps appealed to different people in quite different ways, or it could be that many voters were hard-pressed to know where it stood at all. By 2002 its appeal was, if not very well defined, at least better defined. Green issues had become better absorbed into the mainstream of party politics. The Progressive Democrats have followed a slightly different path. In 1989, the party was closer to Fine Gael than to Fianna Fáil, despite sharing government with the latter in what Fianna Fáil's Brian Cowen described to the party faithful as a 'temporary little arrangement'. After two spells in office with Fianna Fáil, the party seems closer to Fianna Fáil than it once was; at least in 2002 it appears to occupy a space that stretches into that between Fine Gael and Fianna Fáil. At the same time, Sinn Féin has become less well defined. Still on the left, it fits less well there than it did thirteen years earlier. It appears that the nature of party competition is less well defined in 2002 than it was at the end of the 1980s.

This raises the question about the substantive meaning (if there is one) of that space. We have already used the terms 'left' and 'right' in a merely spatial sense, but these terms may also apply when used in a political sense. In 2002 and in 1989, voters were willing to locate themselves on a left–right scale when asked to do so. If we judge parties by their supporters, we would put Sinn Féin on the left, followed by the Greens, Labour, the Progressive Democrats, Fine Gael and Fianna Fáil.[7] This ordering equals the best scale in 1989 and was almost as good as the best in 2002, so we may with some justification talk of the space as a left–right one. What that means in terms of issues is another matter altogether, but the results of some previous analysis suggests that concepts of left and right in Ireland do not have firm connections to contemporary political issues (Garry and Marsh, 2001; also Knutsen, 1995a, 1995b) and, to the extent that they do, issues of morality, such as abortion, are as significant a part of what 'left' and 'right' mean as are economic issues concerning the distribution of wealth and the control of resources. The political parties may stimulate people's self-placements more than political issues. In other words, voters may see themselves as left-orientated because they support Labour, rather than support Labour because they see themselves as left-wing and identify Labour as a party for left-wing people. Certainly, Irish electoral competition has rarely served to emphasize issues in terms of left and right. However, this is a topic requiring further analysis, linking the positions of individual voters in the party space we have described with that of the voters in a space more clearly defined by issues.

## Conclusion

This chapter began by asking to what extent the Irish electorate is now open to electoral competition and, if it is open, how far that competition takes a structured form. Also addressed was the question of whether there has been change in this respect in recent years. Using a set of questions that measure party utilities by asking people about their likelihood of voting for various parties it has been shown that a substantial part of the electorate is very much open to competition and that only a minority of voters seem to be out of competition. A comparison of survey data from 2002 with similar survey data from 1989 provides little evidence of

7. Respondents were also asked to locate the parties. The ordering given by the mean position of each party is the same as that given by using the self-placement of each party's sup-

significant change in this respect. Similar percentages of voters in 2002 and 1989 rated more than one party as being the one for which they were most likely to vote. However, there seems to be evidence of an increase in the percentage of voters who can think of no party they are likely to vote for, a change that parallels the decline in turnout over the period.

This decline in the average level of support for any party means that, in one sense, fewer voters might be said to be in competition, or floating between parties. If competition is not increasing between the parties, it seems to be increasing between the ballot box and the armchair. This certainly gives each party an opportunity to tap into a potential vote that no other party appears to be able to attract. In terms of the structure of competition, clear signs were found of a structure in 2002, into which all parties, if not the independents, could be fitted satisfactorily. This ran from Sinn Féin through Greens, Labour, Progressive Democrats and Fine Gael to Fianna Fáil. When this was compared with the structure in 1989, it became evident that there have been changes in the perception of parties. Sinn Féin seem less clearly identified as being on the extreme left, and the Progressive Democrats are placed marginally closer to Fianna Fáil than they were, while the Greens, previously a marginal fit in any scale, now fit satisfactorily between Sinn Féin and Labour. Certainly, it cannot be said that there is now a stronger one-dimensional structure. If anything, there seemed to be more structure in 1989. Although there is evidence that the public perceives parties as arranged in a left–right ordering that resembles their own left–right self-placement, this structure is not pronounced. Ireland's electoral competition in 1989 was already relatively unstructured in these terms by comparison with other EU countries. In 2002 it seems even more unstructured. Despite the growth of small parties with apparently distinct social and ideological appeals, electoral politics in 2002 looks like a war of all against all.

A caveat should be entered here. The 1989 survey was carried out in the wake of a general election and a European Parliament election, whereas the 2002 survey was conducted a few months before the general election of 2002. It has been shown that election campaigns can increase support for all parties, and that campaigns can serve to sharpen electoral appeals (van der Brug et al., 2000). The 2002 election may well have done that and post-2002 data may show more structure and a larger electorate in competition.

There are obvious avenues for further research. One is to compare the 1989 survey with a post-2002 election survey, which is now available. A second is to explore the link between competition and turnout, and find out whether those who rate no party highly are the very people who are most likely to stay at home on polling day, effectively narrowing the field available for competition between the parties. A third is to explore the substantive meaning (if there is one) of the underlying structures we have described; and a fourth is to examine the social location and issue concerns of the floating voters.

## References

Coombs, C.H. (1975, 2nd edition), *A Theory of Data*. New York/ London: John Wiley.

Garry, J., and M. Marsh (2001), 'Citizens' Conceptions of Left–Right: Religious Context Effects'. Paper presented to ECPR Conference, Canterbury, Sept.

Garry, J., F. Kennedy, M. Marsh and R. Sinnott (2003), 'What Decided the Election?' in M. Gallagher, M. Marsh and P. Mitchell (eds.), *How Ireland Voted 2002*. Basingstoke: Palgrave: 119–41.

Knutsen. O. (1995a), 'Political Conflicts and Left–Right Identification: A Comparative Study', *European Journal of Political Research* 28: 63–93.

Knutsen. O. (1995b), 'Left–Right Materialist Value Orientations', in J. W. van Deth and E. Scarborough (eds.), *The Impact of Values*. Oxford: Oxford University Press: 160–96.

Mair, P. (1987), *The Changing Irish Party System*. London: Frances Pinter.

Oppenhuis, E. V. (1995), *Voting Behaviour in Europe*. Amsterdam: Het Spinhaus.

Tillie, J. (1995), *Party Utility and Voting Behavior*. Amsterdam: Het Spinhuis.

van der Brug, W., C. van der Eijk and M. Marsh (2000), 'Exploring Uncharted Territory: The Irish Presidential Election 1997', *British Journal of Political Science* 30: 631–50.

van der Eijk, C., and M. N. Franklin (eds.) (1996), *Choosing Europe? The European Electorate and National Politics in the Face of Union*. Ann Arbor, MI: The University of Michigan Press.

van der Eijk, C., and K. Niemoller (1983), *Electoral Change in the Nether- lands*. Amsterdam: CT-Press.

van der Eijk, C., and E. V. Oppenhuis (1991), 'European Parties' Per- formance in Electoral Competition', *European Journal of Political Research* 19.1: 55–80.

van Schuur, W. H. (1984), *Structure in Political Beliefs. A New Unfolding Model with Application to European Party Activists*. Amsterdam: CT Press.

van Schuur, W. H. (1988), 'Stochastic Unfolding', in W. E. Saris and I. N. Gallhofer (eds.), *Sociometric Research* 1. *Data Collection and Scaling*. London: Macmillan: 137–58.

# Conclusion

## *Niamh Hardiman*

Economic growth accelerated in the 1990s and Ireland became a very wealthy country by any standards. The bad economic news of the 1980s – emigration, unemployment, massive national debt and high inflation – was replaced by the success stories of employment, growth and stability. Growth rates averaged 8.5 per cent between 1996 and 2000, a level that was almost four times the European average, and Ireland came to enjoy practically full employment (OECD, 2001). This economic success had far-reaching consequences for many areas of life, including, for example, the cultural mix in society, gender roles, the level of economic inequality and the environment.

First and most dramatically perhaps, the face of Irish society changed in a literal sense. The ethnic composition of the population in many cities and towns is now far more diverse than it was a mere two decades ago. Irish economic prosperity attracted people from a wide range of countries around the world and there was a rapid increase in the numbers seeking political asylum. Secondly, the expansion of employment opportunities that came with economic growth has had far-reaching implications for family life. Women at all stages of life have gone out to work in unprecedented numbers and at all skill levels (O'Connell, 2000). Where once Ireland was among the European countries with the lowest numbers of women working – especially married women, and married women with young children even more so – family patterns are now looking very different. Furthermore, more women are having children in situations other than in the traditional household with two married parents (Fahey, 1998; Fahey et al., 2000). Thirdly, while it is true that rising economic prosperity has led to significant increases in living standards for Irish citizens, some citizens have obviously done better than others. High earners have benefited not only from faster-growing incomes but they are also the group that has benefited most from changes in tax policy (Nolan et al., 2002). Thus, while the average material wealth of Irish citizens has increased, there has been a growing disparity between the richest and poorest in society.

A fourth consequence of economic growth relates to the environment. Rapid growth has arguably had a negative impact on the environment and many commentators now argue that further economic development should take place in the context of sustainable growth.

How significant have these changes been? Is Ireland becoming a successful multicultural society, or is it brewing problems of hate crime and racial antagonism? If traditional family patterns of balancing work and home life are changing, what is replacing them? And do men and women feel the same way about what is emerging? In relation to Ireland's new-found wealth and the resulting economic inequality, we may well wonder whether people resent those who have wealth, or want to emulate them. In the new context of national wealth and opportunity, do people blame poverty on the poor, or do citizens favour greater redistribution of wealth? How concerned are Irish people about the detrimental effects that unprecedented levels of economic growth may have on the environment? Do they worry about the despoliation of the natural environment by their collective waste, or do they feel indifferent to nature as something separate from their own concerns?

These are some of the key questions this book has sought to address. To answer them, we asked Irish citizens about their attitudes towards the ethnic composition of their society, gender roles, poverty and wealth, and the natural environment. We have sought to place the findings in the context of a wider consideration of how people's political preferences take shape and what people now expect from the political process. Behind this range of questions are two broader themes that may help us to situate the Irish experience in a wider context of trends across all developed societies. The first theme concerns the role of politics in an increasingly globalized world. The second concerns the ways in which shifting attitudes and values may contribute to the overall quality of the political, social and civic life we share – that is, to the normative bases of civil society.

## Politics in a Globalized World

Much concern has been expressed in Ireland, as in other countries, about the decline in citizens' engagement with politics over the last couple of decades (FitzGerald, 2003). Levels of electoral participation have been falling in most advanced industrial societies. Indeed, in the USA, those who do not vote now routinely outnumber those who do. Perhaps this decline in political engagement is due to the fact that the politics of radical change has gone out of fashion. Even the politics of gradual social change seems to have stalled in many societies. Social democratic parties increasingly find themselves obliged to accept the

basic logic of the market (Kitschelt et al., 1999a). This is due, in significant part, to the liberalization of capital markets since the 1980s
(Cerny, 1993; Garrett, 1998; Simmons, 1999). This development,
together with related technological developments, means that cross-
border capital flows are now so rapid, so unimaginably huge and capable of such dramatic ebbs and flows, that governments everywhere have
to be highly attentive to the opinions of the markets. Market decisions
taken by investors or their agents are frequently based on highly imper-
fect knowledge and information (Strange, 1997). Yet the possibility of
capital flight has been internalized into the decision-making of national
governments everywhere, and political actors have undoubtedly become
more strongly averse to the risk of annoying investors. The end result is
a decline in the plausibility of radical left policies and a muddying of the
traditional distinctions between political parties in terms of left and
right.

What this might mean for democratic politics is contested. A growing
social movement takes a strong stance against globalization. Although
the focus of criticism varies for different groups, a common concern is
the fact that rich countries are much better equipped to engage in the
global market than poor countries (Hirst and Thompson, 1999). The
anti-globalization movement often looks rather distantly related to any
political process, as it tends to be most visible in noisy street protests
against meetings of the G8, the WTO, the IMF and the World Bank, or
at EU summits. Yet implicit in the anti-globalization critique is the
assumption that political decision-making by the wealthiest nations can
and should change the tilt of the global playing field to lessen the inherent bias against poor nations. Anti-globalization critics wish to put
organizations such as the WTO or the IMF under pressure to reform
(Stiglitz, 2002) and hence have a deep faith in the ability of politics to
make a difference.

An alternative analysis would be considerably more pessimistic for the
scope of politics. According to this view, market pressures constrain
democratic politics so tightly that room for meaningful choice is
reduced to almost nothing; the most market-conforming solution is the
one that governments will be required to take if they wish to avoid
unpleasant economic consequences. The logic of this argument is that
governments have little if any discretion about the amount of tax they
raise, how they raise it, the volume of public spending, or the extent of
social welfare support. Governments will all engage in a 'race to the
bottom', in which living standards, the needs of the most vulnerable and
the quality of social services will all be sacrificed in order to maximize
the scope of market activities (see Rodrik, 1997, 2003).

Empirically informed studies do not support this conclusion,
however. It seems that it is still possible to have very different models of

capitalism, in which the configuration of institutions and policies can vary quite widely, while maintaining levels of output, productivity and quality that are globally competitive (Berger and Dore, 1996; Kitschelt et al., 1999a; Hall and Soskice, 2002). Governments still have discretion over tax and spending policies, even if the trade-offs have become more difficult to manage (Esping-Andersen, 1999; Steinmo, 2002). National states retain a vital role as gatekeepers to the globalized economy – and not only in the EU context (Weiss, 1998, 2003). In short, politics remains crucially important to the collective well-being of countries, and to the distribution of income among their citizens.

And yet we see that politics appears to excite relatively little interest among voters, at least if this is measured in terms of the extent of political participation. The issue of what this might mean is of considerable interest to those on all sides of the political spectrum. Liberal commentators tend to be greatly alarmed at the apparent abandonment of political and social responsibility by so many citizens (Putnam 1995, 2001). Others may take some comfort in it on the grounds that the less well educated, who tend to vote least, also have the most intolerant and illiberal attitudes, so selective abstention may be beneficial to the health of democracy (Lipset, 1983). Yet others may put the phenomenon down to rational self-interest; the politics of contentment among the comfortably off majority discourages and marginalizes the rest (Galbraith, 1987).

European welfare states have always been predicated on a more collectivist commitment to the role of the state and its responsibility to citizens. Where political engagement falls off in these societies, commentators are perhaps quicker to anticipate a threat to the viability of democracy itself. So it is important to examine whether and why voters really are alienated from democratic politics altogether, and whether they may as a consequence be available for mobilization into more extreme radical political movements. It is important to find out whether people really believe that governments are completely powerless in the face of global economic forces, that markets will always triumph and that there is no alternative to laissez-faire policies. It is important to identify what sorts of issues and alignments matter most to people in making them feel part, if at all, of the political life of their country.

The findings set out in this book offer more hope for the viability of and prospects for democracy than the sceptics might have feared. Chapter 5 by John Garry shows that about three-quarters of respondents are satisfied with democracy. And far from thinking that politics is redundant, most people think that the government has a lot of power to make a difference to people's lives. People evidently still retain high levels of expectation about what government can do to make the quality of their lives better or worse. That said, the level of engagement with politics clearly varies a lot. Up to half the people surveyed had little or no interest in politics. This pattern is stronger among people with lower levels of education and among women. Far from being a natural consequence of global forces, lower levels of political engagement would, on this evidence, appear to be the result of people's actual experiences with the way political life works. Moreover, people are not alienated from all of public life – there are high levels of trust in institutions such as the civil service, the courts and gárdaí, which would appear to stem from a belief in their integrity and probity. Thus, there may be scope for political parties to build on people's desire for politics to make a difference to their lives. At the moment, identifiable sectors of Irish society clearly feel more disengaged than others, because they do not feel they have a vested interest in the outcomes of the political process. Some of the smaller parties, notably the Greens and Sinn Féin, have begun to capitalize on political disaffection and alienation. A challenge is presented to the larger parties to find workable solutions to the problems that people want politics to address, to engage people more actively with the debate about what needs to be done and how it should be done.

Fiachra Kennedy and Richard Sinnott build upon the earlier work of Sinnott (1995) and Laver and Hunt (1992) in their analysis in Chapter 6 of the issue dimensions around which parties mainly compete. Ireland indeed features a left–right dimension analogous to that of other European countries, and a liberal–authoritarian dimension. In addition, a third issue concerning Northern Ireland traditionally differentiates parties along a nationalist dimension, although there is some evidence that this has weakened since the Good Friday Agreement in 1998. Interestingly, insofar as a clear left–right policy cleavage exists, Kennedy and Sinnott argue that it is relatively incoherent, being made up of two distinct sub-cleavages: attitudes to the market, and attitudes to wealth redistribution.

In Chapter 4, Niamh Hardiman, Tony McCashin and Diane Payne take a different look at economic equality and redistribution. European parties of the left have historically centred much of their appeal on challenging the justice of market distribution. They have invoked a sense of collective concern and communal solidarity to underpin the state's role in the redistribution of resources and opportunities. In the Irish context, it emerges that there is widespread support among all social classes for the principle of individual responsibility in the matter of whether people become rich or remain poor. Yet there is also a widespread belief that the social order is not only very unequal to start with, but also that it is biased in favour of those who start out with advantages. There are class-based differences in the intensity of these views. People who are less well off are most likely to accept that structural factors (as well as individual effort) affect people's circumstances. In other European countries, awareness of the structural basis of people's poverty and wealth provides the basis for mobilization into a left-wing or social democratic view of the world. This chapter concludes that roughly a quarter of respondents hold views that are consistent with such a world view, but that the largest single group, one-third of respondents, hold mixed views that would seem to fit well with the diffuse ideological appeal of Fianna Fáil and Fine Gael.

Party preference is the theme of Chapter 7 by Michael Marsh. He investigates how the support bases of the various Irish parties may overlap, and assesses the extent to which there are 'potential electorates' rather than simply distinct and non-overlapping sets of party supporters. This is quite a nuanced approach to examining party support and allows us to assess the extent to which the electorate is genuinely open to competition between the different parties, and whether there are many genuinely 'floating' voters. Marsh concludes that a substantial part of the electorate is very much open to competition; only a minority of voters seem to be 'out of competition'. Furthermore, although the party system seems somewhat less structured in 2002 compared with 1989, the picture painted by Marsh of the nature of party competition has not fundamentally changed between the two time points, suggesting remarkable durability in the relationship between voters and parties.

## The Normative Bases of Civil Society

There is, of course, no necessary or linear connection between economic growth and changes in values and attitudes. Sociologists used to expect that all societies, as they grew wealthier, would converge upon a single model of modernization. The expectation was that economic growth would result in the decline of organized religion and the widespread secularization of society. Correspondingly, rising education levels would be expected to create a more tolerant, pluralist society. The evidence from across the wealthy democracies does not support these predictions. There is no single model of modernity towards which all societies tend. There is scope for a lot of variation and, while societies change as they become wealthier, the trend and speed of change depends just as much on their starting point and the way they experience change, as on the fact of economic growth (Hardiman and Whelan, 1998).

Yet some quite general shared trends seem to have been emerging across the wealthy societies over recent decades (Crouch, 1999). For example, it seems to be quite common among the wealthier societies for traditional family structures to come under increasing pressure – new educational opportunities, new kinds of jobs, new styles of living and new opportunities for associating with other people in cities all contribute to this. And while secularization turns out to be more complicated than many had expected, the authoritative hold of traditional religious leaders seems everywhere to be loosened by economic growth.

Traditional norms and values tend to be further challenged by the articulation of new preferences and choices by the women's movement. While there is no single explanation for the timing or strength of its emergence, this has been one of the most striking features of change in the values informing public life over recent decades, in Ireland as much as elsewhere (Galligan, 1998). Traditional values had sanctioned a gender-based division of labour in both the household and the labour force, and in differential expectations for work-life, economic earning power and family roles. All these values come into question through pressure of pragmatic adaptation as much as through explicit scrutiny, debate and critique. In summary, while the convergence claims made by modernization theory turn out to be too simple, it is undeniable that underlying the variations in patterns of living among the wealthy democracies there is also a considerable degree of commonality in the direction and significance of social change.

Strong claims have also been made that economic growth introduces value change in the political as well as the societal domain across the wealthy societies. The contention here is that the politics of left and right cease to be as relevant to voters, who are, in the main, materially quite comfortable and secure. The opportunity opens up for new values to structure people's political choices, values that are postmaterialist in nature (Inglehart, 1977, 1990; Dalton et al., 1984). While the politics of the post-war decades centred on managing and sustaining growth and on building up the welfare state, the politics of postmaterialism centres on quality-of-life issues such as participation, self-expression, equality on dimensions such as gender and race that are not directly related to economic issues, and a critique of growth for its own sake. Among these issues is a concern for the natural environment, and Green parties are perhaps the most successful organized expression of the politics of post-materialism.

Comparative studies of the experience of growth in wealthy democracies lead us to expect that Ireland might be displaying similar trends to those apparent elsewhere. We would also, of course, expect to find many distinctively Irish aspects of the attitudes and values we investigate. The dominance of Catholic teaching across a range of personal, familial, social and political aspects of life has been pervasive for most of the lifetime of the independent state and will certainly have left its distinctive residue in the profile of attitudes and values (Inglis, 1998). As late as the early 1990s, weekly church attendance stood at uniquely high levels in comparative terms. The depth of attachment to Catholic practices may not have been all it seemed at the time, since much of it was fairly easily dislodged during the 1990s. By the early twenty-first century, regular church attendance still stood above European averages, but had fallen significantly. It was not modernization per se, but arguably the collapse in the moral authority of the leadership of the Catholic Church that caused this. Nevertheless, there has clearly been a crisis at the public level in what had previously been a widely shared discourse about what mattered and why in personal, familial and social morality. In this book, we have sought to examine how people are making sense of these issues for themselves.

Betty Hilliard's work in Chapter 3 on gender roles and expectations examines similarities and differences in what men and women expect from their closest relationships and from family life. She draws on data from different time points and so we can see whether distinctive trends are observable. She finds that there is definitely evidence for a 'modernization' having taken place of gender roles in Ireland. Women's expectations have clearly moved away from the traditional norms of marriage, followed by full-time mothering and home-making, as the principal life's work of women. Attitudes vary, as might be expected, in relation to age and education.

Ireland is often considered to be a highly familial society, in the sense of valuing family relationships, socializing with family, and depending on family members for assistance at difficult points in the life cycle. These traits are still strongly evident, notwithstanding the considerable shifts in patterns of family formation, especially the growth in non-marital births and in family dissolution. Yet if these can be seen as part of a trend towards 'modernization', Ireland's trajectory is faster than that of Italy, a country with a similarly deep exposure to Catholic socialization patterns, but much slower than that of Britain, its closest geographical neighbour and a society with whose culture Ireland is very familiar.

Familialism, while often acknowledged as a virtue in maintaining strong social bonds and networks in the age of the nuclear family, can also be something of a liability when it comes to generating a sense of belonging to a wider social community. Social analysts have found that societies in which people are very strongly tied to their families do not tend to support a strong sense of civic identity, of voluntary acceptance of obligation to the wider society (Banfield, 1958). By contrast, societies in which people socialize widely with others in any kind of forum, from sporting organizations to choirs, voluntary charity work and school boards, tend to support stronger civic values. This is said to enrich the quality of democratic debate and to facilitate the growth of a better quality of political life (Putnam, 1993, 2001).

One measure of the emergent quality of Irish civic life is based on the attitudes people hold towards the newly diverse composition of the population. Has Ireland become more tolerant, inclusive and pluralist in outlook in the course of becoming more highly educated and wealthier? The work of Michael O'Connell and Nessa Winston in Chapter 1 sets out a rather mixed story. Up to two-thirds of people disavowed any suggestion of racism on their own part. But this also means that about one-third of respondents were prepared to acknowledge that the presence of people of other nationalities or races caused them some discomfort.

Quite what this means may not be evident at first glance. After all, the rate of inward migration from other ethnic groups, while small compared with many other countries, has grown quite rapidly in recent years. It may take Irish people some time to get accustomed to the idea that Ireland is a highly desirable destination for many other people. This also presents a challenge to well-established notions of national identity, traditionally grounded in a story about ethnic homogeneity in which Catholicism, the Irish language and national independence also feature prominently. National identity has been further secured by a sense of smallness, of community, of 'everyone knowing everyone else'. These familiar aspects of national identity can take some time to adjust to the fact that the population has grown more diverse. Supporting this interpretation, over 60 per cent of respondents hoped for the assimilation of minorities as the way forward.

But other aspects of people's attitudes reveal more than a struggle to reconfigure the sense of national identity. O'Connell and Winston report on the growth in the incidence of racially motivated violence and abuse, despite the steady economic growth that should have contributed to defusing the conflicts of economic interest that often help fuel racial tensions elsewhere. They also found a decline in sympathy for political refugees and a growing suspicion that they abuse the system. Hostility was particularly marked towards Nigerians, Muslims and Chinese people. Moreover, Ireland's indigenous ethnic minority, the Travellers, headed the list of most unpopular minorities. These findings suggest that the majority population is as yet far from being at ease with the new diversity in its midst.

Yet the evidence also shows some positive features of adjustment. A large majority of respondents supported better public measures to prevent discrimination and to make life better for minorities in Ireland. This is consistent with other findings, by Hardiman et al. in Chapter 4, that there is considerable support for the rule of law and fair treatment for everyone; and high expectations that government can intervene to make things better.

In Chapter 2, Brian Motherway and Mary Kelly report on another facet of the changing profile of values and attitudes: a concern with the natural environment and environmental issues. In this, they target one of the core elements of the postmaterialist quality-of-life value orientation. They were particularly keen to assess attitudes towards sustainable development, that is, a stance that would accord a consistent and central place for environmental issues alongside economic growth priorities.

Their analysis goes beyond the recurrent controversies about waste management and where to site incinerators and landfill dumps. They find that while the intensity of concern over environmental issues has diminished since 1993, it has become more widely shared across all sectors of the population. They attribute this to the success of environmental activists. In 1993, the relationship between growth and environmental protection was seen as conflictual and as requiring some element of trade-off between the two. This was less evident in the most recent survey, no doubt because economic growth reduced the perceived tensions between competing priorities on each side. But Motherway and Kelly also suggest that the relevance of environmental issues has become more salient for more people. They recognize that environmental issues have many aspects and that effective political leadership needs to be provided constantly, to inform people about a whole range of issues. Too often, this has been left to the experts and the technically well informed. Moreover, it is well known that even where information is widely available and understood, the assessment of risk is extraordinarily difficult (Beck, 1992), and particularly difficult to manage as an issue in local democratic political deliberation. They conclude with an urgent call for wider debate about the many aspects of the natural environment on which we must take collective decisions.

## Conclusion

The attitudes and values we have profiled here relating to ethnic minorities, gender roles, poverty and wealth, and environmental concerns all have a bearing on the wider issues of how we relate to one another, how we treat one another, what we expect of one another. Many of the values we have examined are consistent with what we would expect from a phase of economic growth, occupational diversification and a growing sense of the wider possibilities open to individuals in the choices they make for themselves. Some of our findings offer little comfort to those who would hope for a better quality of community, civic and public life to follow from Ireland's new-found place among the wealthy democracies. Yet we have also seen that a majority of people have very positive expectations about what the political system can and should deliver to improve the quality of citizens' lives.

This does not seem entirely consistent with the decline in political participation, the widespread lack of interest in politics, or the sense many people have that there is little difference between the political parties, and that they as individuals can do little to influence political outcomes. But a number of the authors of this volume have identified a stratum of fundamental values on which people draw when making their judgements. As it comes to terms with the aftermath of economic boom, Irish society faces new challenges and choices, the outcomes of which are likely to have far-reaching implications for the kind of society it becomes over the coming decades. If there is any single, broad conclusion we might draw from the studies in this volume, it is that there may well be a bigger role for political deliberation among the electorate than politicians generally assume. The characteristics of the Irish political system may well seem to reward the diffusion of conflict and avoidance of hard choices. But there would seem to be more scope than may be commonly assumed for political leaders to set out clearly the scope and implications of competing policy choices.

# References

Banfield, E. C. (1958), *The Moral Basis of a Backward Society*. New York: Free Press.

Beck, U. (1992), *Risk Society*. London: Sage.

Berger, S., and R. Dore (eds.) (1996), *National Diversity and Global Capitalism*. Ithaca, NY: Cornell University Press.

Cerny, P. (1993), *Finance and World Politics: Markets, Regimes and States in the Post-Hegemonic Era*. Aldershot: Edward Elgar.

Crouch, C. (1999), *Social Change in Western Europe*. Oxford: Oxford University Press.

Dalton, R., S. Flanagan and P. Beck (eds.) (1984). *Electoral Change in Advanced Industrial Democracies: Realignment or Dealignment?* Princeton, NJ: Princeton University Press.

Esping-Andersen, G. (1999), *Social Foundations of Postindustrial Economies*. Cambridge: Cambridge University Press.

Fahey, T. (1998), 'Progress or Decline? Demographic Change in Political Context', in William Crotty and David E. Schmitt (eds.), *Ireland and the Politics of Change*. Harlow: Addison Wesley Longman: 51–65.

Fahey, T., H. Russell and E. Smyth (2000), 'Gender Equality, Fertility Decline and Labour Market Patterns among Women in Ireland', in B. Nolan, P. J. O'Connell and C. T. Whelan (eds.) (2000), *Bust to Boom? The Irish Experience of Growth and Inequality*. Dublin: Economic and Social Research Institute/Institute of Public Administration: 244–67.

FitzGerald, G. (2003), *Reflections on the Irish State*. Dublin: Irish Academic Press.

Galbraith, J. K. (1987), *The Affluent Society*. London: Penguin, 4th edition.

Galligan, Y. (1998), *Women and Contemporary Politics in Ireland: From the Margins to the Mainstream*. London: Cassell.

Garrett, G. (1998), *Partisan Politics in the Global Economy*. Cambridge: Cambridge University Press.

Hall, P. A., and David Soskice (eds.) (2002), *Varieties of Capitalism*. Cambridge: Cambridge University Press.

Hardiman, N., and C. T. Whelan (1998), 'Changing Values', in William Crotty and David E. Schmitt (eds.), *Ireland and the Politics of Change*. Harlow: Addison Wesley Longman: 66–85.

Hirst, P., and G. Thompson (1999), *Globalization in Question: the International Economy and the Possibilities of Governance*. Cambridge: Polity Press, 2nd edition.

Inglehart, R. (1977), *The Silent Revolution: Changing Values and Political Style among Western Publics*. Princeton, NJ: Princeton University Press.

Inglehart, R. (1990), *Culture Shift in Advanced Industrial Society*. Princeton, NJ: Princeton University Press.

Inglis, T. (1998), *Moral Monopoly: the Rise and Fall of the Catholic Church in Modern Ireland*. Dublin: UCD Press, 2nd edition.

Kitschelt, H., P. Lange, G. Marks and J. D. Stephens (1999a), 'Convergence and Divergence in Advanced Capitalist Democracies', in H. Kitschelt, P. Lange, G. Marks and J. D. Stephens (eds.), *Continuity and Change in Contemporary Capitalism*. Cambridge: Cambridge University Press: 427–60.

Kitschelt, H. (1999b), 'European Social Democracy between Political Economy and Electoral Competition', in H. Kitschelt, P. Lange, G. Marks and J. D. Stephens (eds.), *Continuity and Change in Contemporary Capitalism*. Cambridge: Cambridge University Press.

Laver, M. (1986), 'Ireland: Politics with Some Social Bases: An Interpretation Based on Survey Data', *Economic and Social Review* 17: 193–213.

Laver, M. (1992), 'Are Irish Parties Peculiar?', in J. H. Goldthorpe and C. T. Whelan (eds.), *The Development of Industrial Society in Ireland*. Oxford: Clarendon Press: 359–82.

Laver, M., and W. B. Hunt (1992), *Policy and Party Competition*. London: Routledge.

Lipset, S. M. (1983), *Political Man*. London: Heinemann, 2nd edition.

Nolan, B., B. Gannon, R. Layte, D. Watson, C. T. Whelan and J. Williams (2002), *Monitoring Poverty Trends: Results from the Living in Ireland Surveys*. Dublin: ESRI.

Nolan, B. P., J. O'Connell and C. T. Whelan (eds.) (2000), *Bust to Boom? The Irish Experience of Growth and Inequality*. Dublin: Economic and Social Research Institute/Institute of Public Administration.

O'Connell, P. J. (2000), 'The Dynamics of the Irish Labour Market in Comparative Perspective', in B. P. Nolan, J. O'Connell and C. T.

Whelan (eds.) (2000), *Bust to Boom? The Irish Experience of Growth and Inequality*. Dublin: Economic and Social Research Institute/Institute of Public Administration: 58–89.

OECD (2001), *Economic Surveys: Ireland*. Paris: OECD.

Putnam, R. (1993), *Making Democracy Work: Civic Traditions in Modern Italy*. Princeton, NJ: Princeton University Press.

Putnam, R. (1995), 'Bowling Alone: America's Declining Social Capital', *Journal of Democracy* 6.1: 65–78.

Putnam, R. (2001), *Bowling Alone: The Collapse and Revival of American Community*. New York: Simon and Schuster.

Rodrick, D. (1997), *Has Globalization Gone Too Far?* Institute for International Studies, Washington, DC.

Rodrik, D. (2003), 'Growth Strategies', forthcoming in *Handbook of Economic Growth*; available as PDF document at www.ksg.harvard.edu/rodrik/

Simmons, B. (1999), 'The Internationalization of Capital', in H. Kitschelt, P. Lange, G. Marks and J. D. Stephens (eds.), *Continuity and Change in Contemporary Capitalism*. Cambridge: Cambridge University Press.

Sinnott, R. (1995), *Irish Voters Decide: Voting Behaviour in Elections and Referendums Since 1918*. Manchester: Manchester University Press.

Steinmo, S. (2002), 'Taxation and Globalization: Challenges to the Swedish Welfare State', *Comparative Political Studies* 37: 839–62.

Stiglitz, J. (2002), *Globalization and its Discontents*. London: Penguin.

Strange, S. (1997), *Casino Capitalism*. Manchester: Manchester University Press.

Weiss, L. (1998), *The Myth of the Powerless State: Governing the Economy in a Global Era*. Cambridge: Polity Press.

Weiss, L. (ed.) (2003), *States in the Global Economy: Bringing Domestic Institutions Back In*. Cambridge: Cambridge University Press.

Whyte, J. (1974), 'Politics Without Social Bases', in Richard Rose (ed.), *Electoral Behaviour: A Comparative Handbook*. New York: Free Press.

# Appendix A
# How the survey was conducted

## 1. Background and Target Population

The Irish Social and Political Attitudes Survey was carried out in late 2001/early 2002. The target population for the survey was all adults aged 16 years and over who were living in private households. This explicitly excluded the population in institutions such as long-term geriatric or psychiatric hospitals, old persons' homes, etc. Approximately 2.7 per cent of the total population of the Republic of Ireland are resident in institutions of this sort. A national random sample of the target population was selected as outlined below. All questionnaires were conducted on a personally administered papi basis.

## 2. The Sampling Frame and Sample Design

The only readily available, comprehensive listing of the target population available in Ireland is the electoral register. This provides a list of all adults registered to vote in the state. In selecting the sample for the ISPAS, a three-stage clustered sample design based on the electoral register was used.

In the first instance, a random sample of Primary Sampling Units (PSUs) was selected from the electoral register. [220 District Electoral Divisions (DEDs) were selected as PSUs with an average of 19.9 cases in each]. In the second stage, a random sample of households was selected from within each PSU. In the third stage, a random person was selected in each household.

The sampling frame used for this study was the most up-to-date national electoral register. Electors are recorded in the electoral list in so-called 'Polling Books'. For sample selection purposes, these Polling Books were reconstituted into areal units called District Electoral Divisions. There is a total of 3,400 District Electoral Divisions (DEDs) in Ireland. These DEDs are the most spatially disaggregated areal units in

Ireland for which census data are available and they are the standard PSU building block for random sample selection.

Once the electoral register has been rebuilt into the DED structure, a random sample of PSUs was selected. Each PSU was made up of the DED, or aggregate thereof, using a minimum population threshold criteria. The PSUs were selected with a probability proportionate to size (on a PPS basis).

When the first stage of PSU selection was completed, we selected a sample of households from each one. This was implemented by using a random start and selecting a systematic sample at an appropriate interval, to yield a constant number of households per cluster.

At the third stage of sample selection, we randomly selected a target respondent from each one. This was done using a so-called 'next birthday' rule as a randomizing criterion. In other words, from among all household members who were aged 16 years or over, we selected the person who had the next birthday. To do this. the interviewer simply listed all members of the household aged 16 or more and identified the one who had the next birthday. This 'next birthday' person was the target respondent. No substitution was allowed in cases where that target respondent was unavailable or refused to participate, etc.


### 3.   Split Sample Design

The ISPAS sample was designed in such a way as to carry the instruments for two main surveys: viz. a number of modules – on social justice, the environment, gender roles and racial minorities – as well as the core ISPAS data. To this end, all respondents completed the core ISPAS questionnaire and two of the modules. Half the sample completed the first two modules; and half the sample completed the second two modules. The assignment of target respondents to the different modules of the ISSP was undertaken by filed-management staff in the Head Office of the ESRI – not by the interviewer. The total number of completed questionnaires was 2,529. All 2,529 respondents completed the core ISPAS questionnaire. Additionally, each respondent was handed a 20-minute questionnaire containing a range of additional questions on a variety of topics and asked to fill it in and hand it in to the interviewer or post it to the survey company (ESRI).

## 4.    Response Rates

Table A1  *The total response to the survey for the core ISPAS survey was as outlined below.*

| | All cases | | All contacts | |
|---|---|---|---|---|
| Outcome | No. | % | No. | % |
| Completed | 2,529 | 56% | 2,529 | 58% |
| Refused | 962 | 21% | 962 | 22% |
| Not available throughout fieldwork period | 702 | 15% | 702 | 16% |
| Other | 176 | 4% | 176 | 4% |
| Unable to locate | 147 | 3% | – | – |
| Total | 4,516 | 100% | 4,369 | 100% |

From this table, it is clear that when all target addresses (contacts as well as non-contacts) are considered, the response rate was 56 per cent. When non-contacts are excluded, this increases a little to 58 per cent.

## 4.    Field Procedures

All interviews were completed on a personally administered papi basis. A minimum of five attempted contacts were made with each household in the target sample – an initial contact, plus four callbacks. After an initial contact with anyone in the household, the interviewer continually called back until a definitive outcome in respect of the target respondent was achieved.

Respondents were entered into a closed draw, which has a total of 10 prizes, ranging from IR£1,000 to IR£50 (approximately €1,280 to €64).

The survey was piloted prior to main fieldwork.

## 5.    Weighting the Data

Ex-post weights or grossing factors were applied to the data. These were derived using a minimum information loss algorithm with marginal constraints based on: age; gender; principal economic status; region; marital status; level of educational attainment; household size (number of persons aged 1 year and over). These weights adjust for differences in sample selection probabilities and for differential non-response probabilities according to respondent characteristics.

# Appendix B

## The Economic and Social Research Institute
### 4 Burlington Road Dublin 4 Ph. 6671525

**ESRI** IRISH SOCIAL ATTITUDES SURVEY, WINTER 2001/2002

Interviewer's Name _____

Interviewer's Number [ ][ ][ ]

Area Code [ ][ ]

Respondent Code [ ]

Date of Interview: Day [ ]   Month [ ]

Time Interview Began (24hr clock) [ ][ ][ ]

Introduction to named respondent

**Good morning/afternoon/evening. I am from the Economic and Social Research Institute in Dublin. We have been commissioned by a team of researchers from Trinity College Dublin and University College Dublin to carry out a short survey into social attitudes in Ireland today. You have been selected at random from the Electoral Register to participate in this survey. The interview will take about 55 minutes to complete and all information provided will be treated in the strictest confidence by the Economic and Social Research Institute. It will not be possible for anyone to identify your individual views or attitudes.**

# SECTION A

**A1**  **First of all, I would like to ask you how often you use any of the following media.** [Int. Show Card A1, and tick (✓) one box on each line]

|  | Every day | At least three | At least once times a week | Less often a week | Never |
|---|---|---|---|---|---|
| 1. Newspapers | 53.9 | 19.0 | 19.7 | 4.2 | 3.2 |
| 2. Television | 88.7 | 8.1 | 1.4 | 1.2 | 0.6 |
| 3. Radio | 83.1 | 7.9 | 3.8 | 3.3 | 1.8 |
| 4. Internet | 13.6 | 9.4 | 11.6 | 11.8 | 53.6 |

**A2**  **Which of the following areas do you usually look for in these media?** [Int. Show Card A2 and tick (✓) as many as apply on each row]

|  | News about politics/ economics/ current affairs | Sports, arts and culture or entertainment | Other interests |
|---|---|---|---|
| 1. Newspapers | 69.3 | 67.9 | 32.1 |
| 2. Television | 67.8 | 80.3 | 30.5 |
| 3. Radio | 63.5 | 67.4 | 26.4 |
| 4. Internet | 10.4 | 14.1 | 37.2 |

**A3**  **I will now read out a series of statements. These cover a range of different areas and topics and I would like you to tell me how strongly you Disagree or Agree with each. For each statement I read please tell me whether or not you Strongly Disagree, Disagree, Slightly Disagree, Neither Agree nor Disagree, Slightly Agree, Agree, or Strongly Agree.** [Int. Show card A3, and Please tick (✓) one box on each line]

|  | Strongly Disagree | Disagree Disagree | Slightly Agree nor Disagree | Neither Agree | Slightly | Agree Agree | Strongly |
|---|---|---|---|---|---|---|---|
| 1. Ireland should always follow its own interest, even if this leads to conflicts with other nations | 5.0 | 20.6 | 10.5 | 7.0 | 11.8 | 37.6 | 7.5 |

| | Strongly Disagree | Disagree | Slightly Disagree | Neither Agree nor Disagree | Slightly Agree | Agree | Strongly Agree |
|---|---|---|---|---|---|---|---|
| 1. Ireland should always follow | | | | | | | |
| 2. People should not have to put up with Travellers' halting sites in their neighbourhood | 4.2 | 22.1 | 10.7 | 10.7 | 9.9 | 31.6 | 10.8 |
| 3. God should play a central role in people's lives | 2.2 | 8.3 | 2.6 | 15.4 | 10.8 | 44.8 | 15.9 |
| 4. There is one law for the rich and one for the poor | 3.9 | 14.9 | 4.0 | 5.7 | 12.1 | 43.3 | 16.1 |
| 5. The world would be a better place if people from other countries were more like the Irish | 7.9 | 36.2 | 6.8 | 17.6 | 9.8 | 18.8 | 3.0 |
| 6. It would be better if more people with strong religious beliefs held public office | 9.8 | 40.9 | 8.1 | 15.6 | 6.7 | 15.1 | 3.8 |
| 7. There is nothing wrong with some people being a lot richer than others | 2.5 | 13.8 | 5.5 | 8.0 | 12.2 | 53.7 | 4.2 |

A4    Three issues are outlined on this card. Please tell me for each of the following whether you think it can never be justified, *always* be justified, or something in between. People who believe it can never be justified would give a score of '0'. People who believe it is always justified would give a score of '10'. Other people would place themselves somewhere between these two views. [Int. Show Card A4]

*1. Homosexuality*

Never justified  ————————————————————————→   Always justified

| 0 | 1 | 2 | 3 | 4 | 5 | 6 | 7 | 8 | 9 | 10 |
|---|---|---|---|---|---|---|---|---|---|---|
| 13.0 | 3.2 | 2.7 | 3.9 | 4.3 | 30.9 | 4.9 | 5.2 | 7.0 | 3.7 | 21.3 |

## 2. Abortion

Never justified ————————————————→ Always justified

| 0 | 1 | 2 | 3 | 4 | 5 | 6 | 7 | 8 | 9 | 10 |
|---|---|---|---|---|---|---|---|---|---|----|
| 29.4 | 6.8 | 8.0 | 6.0 | 4.4 | 24.8 | 5.1 | 5.2 | 4.9 | 1.4 | 4.2 |

## 3. Euthanasia (ending the life of those who are terminally ill and wish to die)

Never justified ————————————————→ Always justified

| 0 | 1 | 2 | 3 | 4 | 5 | 6 | 7 | 8 | 9 | 10 |
|---|---|---|---|---|---|---|---|---|---|----|
| 23.5 | 6.9 | 5.3 | 4.2 | 3.4 | 22.0 | 5.6 | 7.1 | 8.5 | 3.1 | 10.3 |

**A5** **On this card I have a number of opposing statements. People who agree fully with the statement on the left would give a score of '0'. People who agree fully with the statement on the right would give a score of '10'. Other people would place themselves somewhere in between these two views. Where would you place yourself on these scales?**
[Int. Show Card A5, and tick (✓) one box on each line]

1. Ireland's membership of the European Union is a **bad** thing ———————————→ Ireland's membership of the European Union is a **good** thing

| 0 | 1 | 2 | 3 | 4 | 5 | 6 | 7 | 8 | 9 | 10 |
|---|---|---|---|---|---|---|---|---|---|----|
| 2.3 | 0.6 | 1.0 | 1.0 | 1.4 | 13.8 | 3.9 | 7.6 | 16.6 | 13.1 | 38.6 |

2. business should be entirely free from State control ———————————→ business should be strictly controlled by the State

| 0 | 1 | 2 | 3 | 4 | 5 | 6 | 7 | 8 | 9 | 10 |
|---|---|---|---|---|---|---|---|---|---|----|
| 15.1 | 5.8 | 7.0 | 7.4 | 6.8 | 34.0 | 7.0 | 5.9 | 3.9 | 1.7 | 4.7 |

3. public or semi-state companies are the best way to provide the services people need → private enterprises are the best way of providing the services people need

| 0 | 1 | 2 | 3 | 4 | 5 | 6 | 7 | 8 | 9 | 10 |
|---|---|---|---|---|---|---|---|---|---|----|
| 3.5 | 9.9 | 5.0 | 5.9 | 5.6 | 29.2 | 9.2 | 8.7 | 8.0 | 4.5 | 10.5 |

4. Ireland should do all it can to unite fully with the European Union → Ireland should do all it can to protect its independence from the European Union

| 0 | 1 | 2 | 3 | 4 | 5 | 6 | 7 | 8 | 9 | 10 |
|---|---|---|---|---|---|---|---|---|---|----|
| 13.8 | 7.3 | 8.4 | 6.6 | 4.6 | 23.6 | 7.8 | 6.2 | 6.4 | 4.5 | 10.8 |

5. there should be more economic growth and jobs even if this means damage to the environment → we should protect the environment even if this means less economic growth and fewer jobs

| 0 | 1 | 2 | 3 | 4 | 5 | 6 | 7 | 8 | 9 | 10 |
|---|---|---|---|---|---|---|---|---|---|----|
| 4.6 | 2.7 | 3.2 | 3.5 | 4.2 | 21.0 | 7.2 | 12.4 | 12.7 | 9.1 | 19.3 |

6. it is essential that all of Ireland becomes united in one state → the different parts of Ireland are best left as separate states

| 0 | 1 | 2 | 3 | 4 | 5 | 6 | 7 | 8 | 9 | 10 |
|---|---|---|---|---|---|---|---|---|---|----|
| 19.2 | 9.0 | 6.1 | 7.2 | 4.7 | 22.0 | 5.0 | 5.9 | 6.3 | 3.4 | 11.1 |

7. most of industry should be State owned and run → most of industry should be privately owned and run

| 0 | 1 | 2 | 3 | 4 | 5 | 6 | 7 | 8 | 9 | 10 |
|---|---|---|---|---|---|---|---|---|---|----|
| 4.6 | 2.5 | 2.1 | 2.3 | 3.0 | 29.1 | 7.3 | 9.7 | 13.4 | 8.5 | 17.5 |

*European unification has already gone too far* → *European unification has not gone far enough*

| 0 | 1 | 2 | 3 | 4 | 5 | 6 | 7 | 8 | 9 | 10 |
|---|---|---|---|---|---|---|---|---|---|---|
| 4.9 | 2.5 | 3.6 | 5.1 | 5.3 | 33.2 | 9.6 | 9.4 | 10.2 | 4.6 | 11.6 |

**A6** **There has been a lot of discussion lately about Irish neutrality. I am interested in finding out what neutrality means. What does Irish neutrality mean to you?**

**A7** **On the whole, are you very satisfied, fairly satisfied, not very satisfied or not at all satisfied with the way democracy works in Ireland?** [Int: Please tick (✓) one box]

| Very satisfied | Fairly satisfied | Not very satisfied | Not at all satisfied | Don't know |
|---|---|---|---|---|
| 8.2 | 60.1 | 18.0 | 7.2 | 6.7 |

**A8** **On the whole, are you very satisfied, fairly satisfied, not very satisfied or not at all satisfied with the way democracy works in the European Union?** [Int: Please tick (✓) one box]

| Very satisfied | Fairly satisfied | Not very satisfied | Not at all satisfied | Don't know |
|---|---|---|---|---|
| 4.3 | 57.9 | 15.4 | 5.0 | 17.4 |

**A9** **I will now read out some more statements. Please tell me to what extent you Disagree or Agree with each statement?** [Int. Show Card A3 and tick (✓) one box on each line].

| | Strongly Disagree | Disagree | Slightly Disagree | Neither Agree nor Disagree | Slightly Agree | Agree | Strongly Agree |
|---|---|---|---|---|---|---|---|
| 1. Sometimes politics and government seem so complicated that a person like me cannot really understand what is going on | 4.8 | 21.4 | 6.9 | 5.9 | 16.7 | 34.9 | 9.4 |

| | Strongly Disagree | Disagree | Slightly Disagree | Neither Agree nor Disagree | Slightly Agree | Agree | Strongly Agree |
|---|---|---|---|---|---|---|---|
| 2. The ordinary person has no influence on politics | 4.0 | 25.9 | 9.6 | 4.1 | 14.5 | 33.9 | 8.0 |
| 3. I think I am better informed about politics and government than most people | 5.9 | 37.0 | 12.7 | 17.0 | 10.4 | 15.0 | 2.0 |
| 4. In today's world, an Irish government can't really influence what happens in this country | 6.1 | 44.3 | 11.9 | 9.3 | 10.0 | 16.2 | 2.2 |
| 5. It doesn't really matter which political party is in power, in the end things go on much the same | 2.3 | 16.9 | 6.0 | 6.0 | 13.4 | 44.9 | 10.4 |
| 6. If a person doesn't care how an election turns out that person should not vote in it | 10.1 | 34.7 | 3.9 | 6.8 | 6.0 | 33.1 | 5.5 |
| 7. The European Union is too complicated to work properly | 2.9 | 34.0 | 11.3 | 21.6 | 12.5 | 15.2 | 2.5 |

**A10** Using **this card please tell me how much you personally trust each of the following. People who *do not trust it at all* would give a score of '0'. People who *trust it a lot* would give a score of '10'. Other people would place themselves somewhere in between these two views. Where would you place yourself on these scales?** [Int. Show Card A6 and tick (✓) one box on each line]

|  | Do not trust at all | | | | | | | | | | Trust a lot |
|---|---|---|---|---|---|---|---|---|---|---|---|
| the Civil Service | 2.5 | 1.4 | 2.6 | 4.2 | 6.7 | 21.3 | 11.2 | 15.4 | 17.5 | 7.1 | 10.0 |
| the Dáil | 9.6 | 4.0 | 7.7 | 8.3 | 9.8 | 24.5 | 11.1 | 10.9 | 7.3 | 2.9 | 3.7 |
| the government | 8.9 | 5.3 | 7.0 | 8.7 | 11.0 | 22.1 | 10.3 | 10.9 | 8.7 | 2.9 | 4.1 |
| the mass media | 9.7 | 6.1 | 10.4 | 11.3 | 14.5 | 22.0 | 8.9 | 6.9 | 5.8 | 2.2 | 2.2 |
| religious leaders | 7.6 | 4.4 | 6.2 | 8.0 | 10.0 | 21.5 | 9.2 | 11.4 | 10.4 | 5.5 | 5.8 |
| the courts | 4.6 | 2.5 | 3.9 | 5.4 | 7.2 | 19.3 | 11.3 | 14.7 | 14.8 | 9.2 | 7.1 |
| the political parties | 11.0 | 6.5 | 9.9 | 10.9 | 14.5 | 25.0 | 7.9 | 6.7 | 4.5 | 1.7 | 1.4 |
| the gardai | 3.9 | 2.0 | 3.0 | 3.5 | 5.5 | 13.3 | 9.4 | 15.5 | 19.7 | 12.8 | 11.5 |
| business leaders | 6.6 | 3.7 | 6.0 | 7.8 | 11.5 | 25.2 | 13.0 | 11.9 | 8.2 | 3.0 | 3.0 |

**A11** I will now read out some statements. Please tell me to what extent you Disagree or Agree with each statement? [Int. Show Card A3 and tick (✓) one box on each line].

|  | Strongly Disagree | Disagree | Slightly Disagree | Neither Agree nor Disagree | Slightly Agree | Agree | Strongly Agree |
|---|---|---|---|---|---|---|---|
| 1. Ordinary working people get their fair share of the nation's wealth | 11.4 | 42.6 | 14.1 | 5.5 | 9.3 | 15.9 | 1.1 |

| | Strongly Disagree | Disagree | Slightly Disagree | Neither Agree nor Disagree | Slightly Agree | Agree | Strongly Agree |
|---|---|---|---|---|---|---|---|
| 2. Income tax should be increased people on higher than for average incomes | 3.2 | 22.3 | 8.4 | 6.9 | 11.7 | 39.0 | 8.5 |
| 3. Generally speaking, Ireland is a better country than most other countries | 0.8 | 7.4 | 4.8 | 11.7 | 14.9 | 51.2 | 9.3 |
| 4. Irish people should support their country even when it is wrong | 8.5 | 47.1 | 10.8 | 10.1 | 6.0 | 15.1 | 2.5 |
| 5. Asylum seekers should have the same rights to social services as Irish people | 6.9 | 23.0 | 12.9 | 9.4 | 13.5 | 30.6 | 3.7 |
| 6. There should be very strict limits on the number of immigrants coming to live in Ireland | 2.5 | 8.9 | 5.9 | 5.1 | 15.6 | 42.9 | 18.9 |
| 7. I would rather be a citizen of Ireland than of any other country in the world | 1.5 | 4.9 | 2.3 | 8.3 | 5.0 | 49.9 | 28.1 |

A12  Do you usually think of yourself as close to any particular political party?

Yes  25.0 → go to A13b      No  72.7 → go to A13a      Don't know  2.3 → go to A13a

A13a  If NO, or Don't Know do you feel yourself a little closer to one of the political parties than the others?

Yes  29.1 → go to A13b      N  64.5 → go to A14a      Don't know  6.4 → go to A14a

**A13b  If YES at A12 or A13a Which party do you feel closest to?…Record name of the party**

**A13c  Do you feel yourself to be very close to this party, somewhat close to this party or not very close to this party?**

Very Close   11.1          Somewhat Close   46.0          Not Very Close   42.2          Don't Know   0.7

**A14a  For one reason or another, a lot of people didn't vote in the last general election. How about you – did you vote?**

Yes   69.5 → go to14b          No   30.5 → go to A14c

**A14b**  [Int: If 'Yes' at A14a ask:]  **Which party did you give your first preference vote to?** [Tick (✓) one box below]

**OR**

**A14c**  [Int: If 'No' at A14a ask:] Suppose you had voted? Which party would you have given your first preference vote to? [Int. Please tick (✓) one box only]

|  | *(did/would)* |  | *(did/would)* |
|---|---|---|---|
| Fianna Fáil | 45.6/25.5 | Sinn Féin | 2.7/6.0 |
| Fine Gael | 21.3/8.9 | Other | 1.0/0.9 |
| Green Party | 2.5/5.4 | Independent | 5.6/3.8 |
| Labour | 9.3/4.8 | Don't know | 8.6/43.2 |
| Progressive Democrats | 3.4/1.4 |  |  |

**A15  If there was a general election tomorrow, to which party would you give your first preference vote?** [Int. Please tick (✓) one box only]

| Fianna Fáil | 35.7 | Sinn Féin | 5.0 |
|---|---|---|---|
| Fine Gael | 14.4 | Independent | 3.9 |
| Green Party | 4.7 | Don't know | 21.6 |
| Labour | 6.6 | I wouldn't vote | 5.4 |
| Progressive Democrats | 2.7 |  |  |

A16  As you may know, there was a referendum on the European Union Nice Treaty last June. There will be another referendum on the Nice Treaty sometime in the next year.

I'd like you to imagine that you are voting on the next referendum on the Nice Treaty. Where would you place yourself on a scale of 1 to 7? A score of '1' means that you would definitely vote *in favour* of the Nice Treaty, and a score of '7' means that you would definitely vote *against* the Nice Treaty. [Int. Show Card A7 and tick (✓) one box only]

*Definitely vote*
***in favour*** *of the*
*Nice Treaty*

*Definitely vote*
***against*** *the*
*Nice Treaty*

| 1 | 2 | 3 | 4 | 5 | 6 | 7 |
|---|---|---|---|---|---|---|
| 23.2 | 7.2 | 6.9 | 29.0 | 7.8 | 6.4 | 19.4 |

A17  Also, there's some talk these days about having a referendum to strengthen the ban on abortion in the constitution. Now I would like you to imagine that you are voting in such a referendum. Where would you place yourself on a scale of 1 to 7? A score of '1' means that you would definitely vote *in favour* of strengthening the ban on abortion a score of '7' means that you would definitely vote *against* strengthening the ban on abortion. [Int. Show Card A7 and tick (✓) one box only]

*Definitely vote in*
***favour*** *of strengthening*
*the ban on abortion*

*Definitely vote*
***against*** *strengthening*
*the ban on abortion*

| 1 | 2 | 3 | 4 | 5 | 6 | 7 |
|---|---|---|---|---|---|---|
| 27.9 | 7.5 | 5.9 | 17.1 | 8.2 | 8.9 | 24.5 |

**A18**  We have a number of political parties in Ireland each of which would like to get your vote. How probable is it that you will ever give your first preference vote to the following parties? Please use the numbers on this scale to indicate your views, where '1' means *Not at all probable* and '10' means *Very probable*. [Int. Show Card A8 and tick (✓) one box on each line]

How probable is it that you will ever give your first preference vote to...

| | Not at all Probable | | | | | | | | | Very Probable |
|---|---|---|---|---|---|---|---|---|---|---|
| Fianna Fáil | 21.0 | 4.5 | 4.7 | 3.9 | 12.2 | 4.9 | 7.2 | 7.6 | 5.6 | 28.3 |
| Fine Gael | 26.6 | 6.6 | 6.7 | 6.8 | 17.0 | 6.9 | 8.0 | 5.8 | 3.6 | 11.9 |
| Green Party | 28.5 | 8.8 | 7.6 | 6.9 | 17.5 | 6.3 | 6.6 | 7.0 | 3.5 | 7.3 |
| Labour | 26.6 | 8.3 | 8.3 | 8.8 | 17.3 | 6.9 | 7.0 | 5.5 | 4.4 | 6.9 |
| Progressive Democrats | 31.2 | 8.9 | 10.0 | 7.9 | 17.3 | 7.2 | 5.9 | 4.5 | 3.0 | 4.1 |
| Sinn Féin | 48.6 | 10.3 | 7.5 | 5.0 | 10.8 | 4.0 | 3.5 | 2.5 | 2.3 | 5.4 |
| An Independent candidate | 22.3 | 5.6 | 4.8 | 5.3 | 19.0 | 7.9 | 8.9 | 8.8 | 6.3 | 11.1 |

**A19**  How interested would you say you are in politics – are you: [Int. Please tick (✓) one box only]

Very interested  11.7     Somewhat interested  42.0     Not very interested  28.5     Not at all interested  17.7

**A20a**  What do you think about the state of the economy in Ireland these days? Would you say that the state of the economy is very good, good, neither good nor bad, bad or very bad? [Int. Please tick (✓) one box only]

Very good  10.7     Good  57.2     Neither good nor bad  24.8     Bad  4.7     Very bad  0.9     Don't Know  1.7

**A21** Would you say that over the last twelve months, the state of the economy in Ireland has got better, stayed the same or got worse? [Int. Please tick (✓) one box only]

Got better  13.7          Stayed the same  31.4 → go to A24          Got worse  52.1          Don't Know  2.9 → go to A24

**A22** Would you say much better or somewhat better?

Much Better  33.6          Somewhat Better  66.4

**A23** Would you say much worse or somewhat worse?

Much Worse  13.2          Somewhat Worse  86.8

**A24** What about your own economic situation these days? Would you say it is.....[Int. Please tick (✓) one box only]

Very good  8.8          Fairly good  77.1          Fairly bad  11.9          Very bad  2.2

**A25** Do you ever stay at home at night because you are afraid of being a victim of crime? [Int. Please tick (✓) one box only]

Yes often  4.7          Yes occasionally  8.1          No  87.3

**A26** Have you or anyone you know been a victim of a crime recently? [Int. Please tick (✓) one box only]

Yes, me  5.5          Yes, someone I know  29.3          Yes, me AND someone I know  2.7          No  62.5

**A27** Which of these two statements comes closest to your view? [Int. Please tick (✓) one box only]

Most people can be trusted  36.1          OR          You can't be too careful in dealing with people  61.0          Don't know  2.9

**A28** How often do you spend time with other people in clubs or associations, religious organisations or voluntary groups of one kind or another? [Int. Please tick (✓) one box only]

Several times a week  22.2          About once a week  25.2          About twice a month  11.0          A few times a year  14.2          Rarely/never  27.4

**A29** Interviewer Record Time (24 hour clock)

# SECTION B  GENDER

**B1**   I will now read out a series of statements to you. I would like you to tell me how strongly you Agree or Disagree with each. For each statement I read please tell me whether or not you **Strongly Agree, Agree, Neither Agree nor Disagree, Disagree, Strongly Disagree.** [Int. Show Card B1 and tick (✓) one box on each line]

| | Strongly Agree | Agree | Neither Agree Nor Disagree | Disagree | Strongly Disagree | Can't Choose |
|---|---|---|---|---|---|---|
| 1. A working mother can establish just as warm and secure a relationship with her children as a mother who does not work. | 13.4 | 46.1 | 7.4 | 22.2 | 7.8 | 3.2 |
| 2. A pre-school child is likely to suffer if his or her mother works. | 3.9 | 30.4 | 12.9 | 38.0 | 11.3 | 3.4 |
| 3. All in all, family life suffers when the woman has a full-time job. | 5.4 | 31.2 | 13.1 | 35.4 | 11.6 | 3.3 |
| 4. A job is all right, but what most women really want is a home and children | 4.1 | 32.8 | 14.8 | 32.1 | 11.3 | 5.0 |
| 5. Being a housewife is just as fulfilling as working for pay | 6.5 | 39.1 | 16.5 | 23.4 | 8.0 | 6.4 |
| 6. Having a job is the best way for a woman to be an independent person | 8.8 | 47.5 | 14.3 | 20.3 | 4.8 | 4.3 |
| 7. Both the man and woman should contribute to the household income | 12.9 | 54.8 | 15.7 | 12.0 | 1.9 | 2.8 |

| | | | | | |
|---|---|---|---|---|---|
| 8. A man's job is to get money; a woman's job is to look after the home and family | 2.4 | 14.7 | 41.2 | 26.2 | 2.7 |
| 9. Men ought to do a larger share of household work than they do now | 12.2 | 55.2 | 10.5 | 2.6 | 2.5 |
| 10. Men already do as much household work as their time permits | 2.3 | 28.6 | 35.9 | 11.5 | 4.0 |

**B2** **Do you think that women should work outside the home Full-time, Part-time or Stay at home under the following circumstances?** [Int: Show Card B2 and tick (✓) one box on each line].

| | Work Full-time | Work Part-time | Stay at home | Can't Choose |
|---|---|---|---|---|
| 1. After marrying and before there are children | 76.4 | 9.1 | 3.0 | 11.6 |
| 2. When there is a child under school age | 8.9 | 43.4 | 34.5 | 13.2 |
| 3. After the youngest child starts school | 22.6 | 55.0 | 9.5 | 12.8 |
| 4. After the children leave home | 64.9 | 18.8 | 2.2 | 14.0 |

**B3** **I am now going to read out a series of statements regarding marriage. For each statement I read please tell me whether or not you Strongly Agree, Agree, Neither Agree nor Disagree, Disagree, Strongly Disagree.** [Int. Show Card B1 and tick (✓) one box on each line]

| | Strongly Agree | Agree | Neither Agree Nor Disagree | Disagree | Strongly Disagree | Can't Choose |
|---|---|---|---|---|---|---|
| 1. Married people are generally happier than unmarried people | 4.2 | 25.2 | 25.0 | 33.0 | 6.2 | 6.4 |
| 2. It is better to have a bad marriage than no marriage at all. | 1.2 | 3.7 | 3.4 | 52.8 | 35.6 | 3.4 |

| Statement | | | | | | |
|---|---|---|---|---|---|---|
| 2. It is better to have a bad marriage than no marriage at all. | 1.2 | 3.7 | 3.4 | 52.8 | 35.6 | 3.4 |
| 3. People who want children ought to get married | 8.1 | 43.0 | 11.0 | 30.2 | 4.8 | 2.9 |
| 4. One parent can bring up a child as well as two parents together | 4.6 | 39.2 | 13.0 | 33.6 | 6.2 | 3.4 |
| 5. It is all right for a couple to live together without intending to get married | 9.3 | 53.5 | 11.1 | 17.4 | 5.8 | 2.9 |
| 6. It's a good idea for a couple who intend to get married to live together first | 10.6 | 52.4 | 14.9 | 15.1 | 4.1 | 3.0 |
| 7. Divorce is usually the best solution when a couple can't seem to work out their marriage problems | 6.8 | 49.3 | 16.6 | 19.7 | 2.1 | 5.5 |
| 8. Watching children grow up is life's greatest joy | 23.0 | 56.0 | 10.8 | 3.0 | 0.7 | 6.5 |
| 9. People who have never had children lead empty lives | 2.2 | 11.0 | 12.4 | 53.7 | 15.9 | 4.9 |
| 10. Working women should receive paid maternity leave when they have a baby | 23.7 | 67.7 | 3.6 | 1.9 | 0.8 | 2.3 |
| 11. Families should receive financial benefits for child care when both parents work | 11.5 | 49.7 | 13.5 | 17.6 | 3.5 | 4.2 |

**B4a** **Do you live with a spouse or partner?**  Yes  54.1 → go to B4b  No  45.9 → go to B12

**B4b** **How do you and your spouse/partner organise the income that one or both of you receive? Please choose the option that comes closest** [Int: Show Card B3 and tick (✓) ONE box only].

| | |
|---|---|
| I manage all the money and give my spouse/partner his/her share | 11.6 |
| My spouse/partner manages all the money and gives me my share | 11.7 |
| We pool all the money and each take out what we need | 54.8 |
| We pool some of the money and keep the rest separate | 13.8 |
| We each keep our own money separate | 8.1 |

**B5** **In your household who mostly does the following things?** [Int: Show Card B4 and tick (✓) one box on each line].

| | Always me | Usually me | About Equal or Both together | Usually my spouse/ partner | Always my spouse/ partner | Is Done by a Third person | Can't Choose |
|---|---|---|---|---|---|---|---|
| 1. The laundry | 34.5 | 12.9 | 10.7 | 16.8 | 23.1 | 1.7 | 0.3 |
| 2. Makes small repairs around the house | 20.9 | 27.5 | 21.1 | 17.4 | 16.6 | 5.1 | 0.3 |
| 3. Cares for sick family members | 21.0 | 13.0 | 37.3 | 11.4 | 10.0 | 1.3 | 6.0 |
| 4. Shops for groceries | 26.8 | 14.6 | 30.1 | 13.6 | 13.7 | 0.8 | 0.4 |
| 5. The cleaning | 23.9 | 16.5 | 26.1 | 14.6 | 14.8 | 3.2 | 0.8 |
| 6. Prepares the meals | 24.7 | 19.0 | 22.5 | 17.2 | 15.3 | 0.9 | 0.3 |

**B6** On average, how many hours a week do you personally spend on household tasks? _____ **hours per week**

**B7** On average, how many hours a week does your spouse/partner, spend on household tasks? _____ **hours per week**

**B8** How often do you and your spouse/partner disagree on your division of household tasks?

| Several times per week | Several times per month | Several times a year | Less often/ rarely | Never | Can't Choose |
|---|---|---|---|---|---|
| 5.7 | 7.4 | 11.2 | 35.6 | 37.3 | 2.7 |

**B9** Which of the following best applies to the division of household work between you and your spouse/partner? [Int: Show Card B5 and tick (✓) one box only].

| | |
|---|---|
| I do much more than my fair share of the household tasks | 18.1 |
| I do a bit more than my fair share of the household tasks | 16.2 |
| I do roughly my fair share of the household tasks | 45.2 |
| I do a bit less than my fair share of the household tasks | 13.8 |
| I do much less than my fair share of the household tasks | 6.7 |

**B10** When you and your spouse/partner make decisions about the following, who has the final say? [Int: Show Card B6 and tick (✓) one box on each line].

| | Mostly Me | Mostly my spouse/partner | Sometimes me/ sometimes my Spouse/partner | We decide together | Someone else |
|---|---|---|---|---|---|
| 1. Choosing weekend activities | 10.3 | 10.0 | 23.6 | 55.7 | 0.3 |
| 2. Buying major things for the home | 12.6 | 11.0 | 13.3 | 62.5 | 0.6 |
| 3. Making social invitations | 12.6 | 12.3 | 15.0 | 59.9 | 0.3 |

**B11** Considering all sources of income (including wages, salaries, pensions, unemployment benefits, income from interest, etc.), between you and your partner, who has the higher income? [Int: Please tick (✓) one box only].

| | |
|---|---|
| I have a much higher income | 30.5 |
| I have a bit higher income | 10.3 |
| We have about the same income | 17.5 |
| My spouse/partner has a bit higher income | 16.2 |
| My spouse/partner has a much higher income | 25.4 |

**B12 To what extent do you Agree or Disagree with the following statements?** [Int: Show Card B7 and tick (✓) one box on each line].

| | Strongly Agree | Agree | Neither Agree Nor Disagree | Disagree | Strongly Disagree | Can't Choose | Doesn't Apply |
|---|---|---|---|---|---|---|---|
| 1. There are so many things to do at home, I often run out of time before I get them all done | 9.2 | 40.8 | 7.7 | 24.9 | 4.1 | 1.1 | 12.1 |
| 2. My life at home is often stressful | 2.2 | 21.4 | 8.8 | 47.4 | 13.0 | 0.6 | 6.6 |
| 3. There are so many things to do at work I often have to put in extra hours | 4.8 | 27.6 | 4.8 | 22.8 | 4.0 | 0.9 | 35.1 |
| 4. My job is often stressful | 4.8 | 31.0 | 6.6 | 19.8 | 3.7 | 0.9 | 33.2 |

**B13 How often has each of the following happened to you during the past three months?** [Int: Show Card B8 and tick (✓) one box on each line].

| | Several times a week | Several times a month | Several times a year | Less Often/ rarely | Never | Doesn't apply/as no job |
|---|---|---|---|---|---|---|
| 1. I have come home from work too tired to do some of the chores which need to be done | 8.8 | 17.7 | 8.6 | 15.0 | 11.5 | 38.4 |
| 2. It has been difficult for me to fulfil my family responsibilities because of the amount of time I spent on my job | 2.8 | 7.1 | 5.7 | 17.1 | 24.3 | 43.0 |
| 3. I have arrived at work too tired to function well because of the household tasks I have done | 0.4 | 1.5 | 2.9 | 13.4 | 39.7 | 42.0 |

4. I have found it difficult to concentrate at work because of my family responsibilities

| | | | | | |
|---|---|---|---|---|---|
| 0.6 | 2.2 | 4.2 | 13.8 | 36.2 | 43.0 |

**B14** **How satisfied are you in your (main) job?** [Int: Show Card B9 and tick (✓) one box only].

| Completely satisfied | Very satisfied | Fairly satisfied | Neither Satisfied nor dissatisfied | Fairly dissatisfied | Very dissatisfied | Completely dissatisfied | Can't choose |
|---|---|---|---|---|---|---|---|
| 13.3 | 29.9 | 36.7 | 5.3 | 2.9 | 1.7 | 0.2 | 10.1 |

**B15** **If you were to consider your life in general these days, how happy or unhappy would you say you are, on the whole?** [Int: Please tick (✓) one box only].

| Very happy | Fairly happy | Not so happy | Not at all happy | Can't choose |
|---|---|---|---|---|
| 42.1 | 52.5 | 2.9 | 0.7 | 1.8 |

**B16** **All things considered, how satisfied are you with your family life as a whole?** [Int: Show Card B9 tick (✓) one box only].

| Completely Satisfied | Very satisfied | Fairly satisfied | Neither satisfied nor dissatisfied | Fairly dissatisfied | Very dissatisfied | Completely dissatisfied | Can't choose |
|---|---|---|---|---|---|---|---|
| 22.1 | 42.4 | 29.8 | 2.1 | 1.1 | 0.2 | 0.2 | 2.2 |

**B17** **Did your mother ever work for pay for as long as one year after you were born and before you were 14?** [Int: Please tick (✓) one box only].

| Yes, she worked | No | Did not live with mother/mother dead |
|---|---|---|
| 27.2 | 70.6 | 2.1 |

**B18** Could I ask you whether or not you have had any children?

| Yes | No |
|---|---|
| 57.1 | 42.9 → go to B21 |

**B19** Did you work outside the home full-time, part-time, or not at all. [Int: Show Card B10 and tick (✓) one box on each line].

|  | Worked Full-time | Worked Part-time | Stayed Home | Does Not Apply |
|---|---|---|---|---|
| 1. After marrying and before you had children | 67.8 | 6.4 | 17.4 | 8.4 |
| 2. And what about when a child was under school age | 46.8 | 13.0 | 34.8 | 5.4 |
| 3. After the youngest child started school | 42.7 | 14.3 | 27.7 | 15.4 |
| 4. And how about after the children left home | 31.1 | 9.0 | 18.8 | 41.1 |

**B20** What about your spouse/partner at that time – did he or she work outside the home full-time, part-time, or not at all? [Int: Show Card B10 and tick (✓) one box on each line].

|  | Worked Full-time | Worked Part-time | Stayed Home | Does Not Apply |
|---|---|---|---|---|
| 1. After marrying and before you had children? | 74.3 | 5.9 | 11.4 | 8.4 |
| 2. And what about when a child was under school age? | 58.5 | 9.6 | 23.1 | 8.8 |
| 3. After the youngest child started school | 52.3 | 11.0 | 19.0 | 17.7 |
| 4. And how about after the children left home | 40.3 | 5.7 | 11.5 | 42.5 |

**B21** Interviewer Record Time (24 hour clock)

# SECTION C  SOCIAL JUSTICE

C1    In Ireland today some people are very well off. For example, they own large houses, expensive cars, have lots of money to spend on luxuries and can save and build up their wealth. Other people are very badly off. They need Social Welfare money to get by, they struggle to pay essential bills like rent and ESB and they have no money left over at the end of the week. I am going to read out a list of statements that people might make to explain why some people are very well-off and some very badly off.

For each of these statements I would like you to tell me how strongly you Disagree or Agree with each. [Int Show Card C1 and tick (✓) one box on each line].

| | Strongly Disagree | Disagree | Slightly Disagree | Neither Agree nor Disagree | Slightly Agree | Agree | Strongly Agree |
|---|---|---|---|---|---|---|---|
| 1. The people who are badly off just waste the money they have | 9.4 | 43.9 | 9.0 | 10.8 | 11.8 | 13.5 | 1.6 |
| 2. The only people who can make a lot of money are the people with the right connections | 3.0 | 31.6 | 8.5 | 6.9 | 17.3 | 28.2 | 4.4 |
| 3. Some people just don't make the effort to help themselves | 1.0 | 9.6 | 5.9 | 6.7 | 24.7 | 46.5 | 5.6 |
| 4. The Government does not give enough money to people on Social Welfare | 2.3 | 22.1 | 10.4 | 16.3 | 15.4 | 27.7 | 5.8 |
| 5. To become very well-off you have to start out with some money to begin with | 2.6 | 25.0 | 6.3 | 6.1 | 14.4 | 40.6 | 5.1 |

| | Strongly Disagree | Disagree | Slightly Disagree | Neither Agree nor Disagree | Slightly Agree | Agree | Strongly Agree |
|---|---|---|---|---|---|---|---|
| 6. People with talent or ability will always make money | 1.5 | 17.5 | 7.9 | 7.1 | 15.0 | 46.3 | 4.8 |
| 7. Hard work is what makes the difference between making a lot of money and making very little | 1.6 | 15.0 | 6.1 | 7.3 | 14.6 | 47.5 | 8.0 |
| 8. Owning your own business rather than being an employee is the way to become really well-off | 1.6 | 16.7 | 6.5 | 13.1 | 14.5 | 37.0 | 10.7 |
| 9. You have to be dishonest to make a lot of money | 14.2 | 53.6 | 7.4 | 6.0 | 8.8 | 8.5 | 1.5 |
| 10. The people with no money are the ones who don't have the kind of qualifications that are needed these days | 3.3 | 34.4 | 8.6 | 11.4 | 16.1 | 24.4 | 1.8 |
| 11. Employers just don't pay enough money to some workers | 0.6 | 6.9 | 4.3 | 8.9 | 17.2 | 54.4 | 7.7 |

**C2** Some people say that poor people are poor because they don't work hard enough. **Others would say that they are poor because of circumstances beyond their control. What do you think? Please indicate where you would place your views on the following scale (choose any number between 0 and 10)** [Int. Show Card C2]

| Most poor people are poor because they don't work hard enough | | | | | | | | | Most poor people are poor because of circumstances beyond their control → | |
|---|---|---|---|---|---|---|---|---|---|---|
| 0 | 1 | 2 | 3 | 4 | 5 | 6 | 7 | 8 | 9 | 10 |
| 0.5 | 0.5 | 1.3 | 1.6 | 1.9 | 15.3 | 9.3 | 15.5 | 20.2 | 13.5 | 20.3 |

**C3a** **The Government has recently set out a legal minimum wage – a minimum rate of pay that workers are entitled to by law. Some people think this is a good idea and some don't. I would like to know your opinion. Please say which one of these two statements comes closest to your opinion.**

I think that a legal minimum wage is a good idea          94.9 → go to C3b

I do not think there should be a legal minimum wage          5.1 → go to C4

**C3b** **You've said that you agree with a minimum wage. Thinking now about adults (people aged 21 and over), what in your opinion would be a fair minimum hourly wage for a full week's work? (Ignore overtime, bonuses, shift allowances, etc.) Please select the figure on the card that comes nearest the figure you have in mind.** [Int: Show Card C3]

*£ Per Hour*

£2.50 per hr.   0.3      £3.50 per hr.   1.3      £4.50 per hr.   13.1      £5.50 per hr.   39.8      £6.50 per hr.   45.4

**C4** I would like to ask you now about differences in the wage or salary for different types of jobs. **Please indicate how much you Disagree or Agree with these statements about what should affect employees' pay.** [Int Show Card C1 and tick (✓) one box on each line].

| | Strongly Disagree | Disagree | Slightly Disagree | Neither Agree nor Disagree | Slightly Agree | Agree | Strongly Agree |
|---|---|---|---|---|---|---|---|
| 1. Jobs that require a high level of qualifications should be more highly rewarded than jobs that don't | 0.4 | 4.5 | 3.0 | 4.7 | 14.7 | 63.3 | 9.5 |
| 2. People doing jobs that have unpleasant working conditions like noise, dirt and smells should be compensated for this | 0.2 | 3.2 | 1.4 | 4.8 | 12.6 | 66.5 | 11.3 |
| 3. People with a lot of responsibility should be paid a lot more | 0.0 | 2.8 | 0.9 | 3.5 | 14.8 | 65.2 | 12.8 |
| 4. If there are shortages of workers for particular jobs employers should pay above the going rate to get workers | 0.4 | 8.8 | 3.8 | 10.3 | 17.1 | 54.6 | 5.1 |
| 5. People in office and administrative work should be paid more than people doing work with their hands | 9.5 | 54.6 | 9.9 | 15.8 | 4.4 | 5.1 | 0.7 |
| 6. Every worker – no matter what his/her job – should get a decent wage even if the firm or organisation is not doing well | 0.3 | 8.4 | 7.3 | 9.1 | 13.6 | 53.8 | 7.5 |

| | Strongly Disagree | Disagree | Slightly Disagree | Neither Agree nor Disagree | Slightly Agree | Agree | Strongly Agree |
|---|---|---|---|---|---|---|---|
| 7. People with families to support should be paid more than those who don't have families to support | 4.5 | 42.6 | 8.1 | 13.6 | 8.6 | 19.0 | 3.4 |
| 8. Employees who consistently produce more or are more efficient than others should get a higher wage | 0.1 | 7.9 | 3.3 | 8.8 | 19.4 | 54.7 | 5.8 |
| 9. Employees with long years of service should get higher pay than other employees who produce the same amount | 2.1 | 24.9 | 7.2 | 11.6 | 19.6 | 32.0 | 2.6 |

**C5** **I am now going to read out a few statements on income differences in Ireland today. Please indicate how much you Disagree or Agree with each. [Int Show Card C1 and tick (✓) one box on each line].**

| | Strongly Disagree | Disagree | Slightly Disagree | Neither Agree nor Disagree | Slightly Agree | Agree | Strongly Agree |
|---|---|---|---|---|---|---|---|
| 1. Everybody in Ireland is much better off now than 5 years ago | 1.0 | 11.6 | 5.3 | 6.2 | 18.7 | 47.7 | 9.5 |
| 2. The poor are getting left behind | 1.2 | 12.0 | 11.7 | 8.1 | 21.6 | 40.0 | 5.3 |
| 3. The incomes of well-off people are rising much faster than anyone else's | 0.2 | 4.4 | 2.5 | 9.5 | 15.9 | 54.6 | 12.8 |
| 4. The ordinary person's income is not much better now than 5 years ago | 2.0 | 33.9 | 15.8 | 8.3 | 12.2 | 25.5 | 2.3 |
| 5. There is no real poverty left now | 14.0 | 47.8 | 14.4 | 5.6 | 7.4 | 9.6 | 1.1 |

**C6** I would like to ask you about people's opportunities in life in Ireland today- whether everybody has an equal chance or not. Please tell me how much you Disagree or Agree with the following statements. [Int Show Card C1 and tick (✓) one box *on each line*].

| | Strongly Disagree | Disagree | Slightly Disagree | Neither Agree nor Disagree | Slightly Agree | Agree | Strongly Agree |
|---|---|---|---|---|---|---|---|
| 1. Everybody has an equal chance to get on | 4.3 | 27.9 | 12.2 | 4.7 | 11.0 | 37.0 | 2.9 |
| 2. Everybody gets rewarded for their effort and hard work | 3.2 | 36.4 | 14.5 | 6.1 | 13.1 | 24.5 | 2.3 |
| 3. Ordinary workers and their families don't have the same opportunities as well-off people | 0.9 | 15.0 | 6.5 | 6.5 | 18.8 | 47.5 | 4.9 |
| 4. If a child from a low-income family gets a good education he or she will get on as well as any other child | 0.8 | 6.3 | 6.0 | 3.7 | 12.5 | 60.7 | 9.9 |
| 5. You can't really have equal opportunities because in the end it all comes down to what social class your are from | 4.7 | 30.8 | 13.2 | 8.9 | 18.3 | 21.0 | 3.0 |

**C7** Now I would like to read out some statements about wealth in Ireland and how it should be shared. Please tell me how much you Disagree or Agree with each. [Int: Show Card C1 and tick (✓) one box on each line].

| | Strongly Disagree | Disagree | Slightly Disagree | Neither Agree nor Disagree | Slightly Agree | Agree | Strongly Agree |
|---|---|---|---|---|---|---|---|
| 1. If people are very wealthy they should be allowed to pass on their wealth to their children without the government taking some of the wealth in taxes | 1.6 | 15.9 | 5.8 | 6.5 | 8.7 | 47.0 | 14.6 |
| 2. As long as there is equal opportunity for all it is fair if some people have more money or wealth than others | 0.3 | 5.2 | 2.4 | 7.7 | 13.3 | 65.1 | 6.0 |
| 3. The government should keep taxes low to encourage people to work and use their skills even if this means greater differences in income between people | 0.7 | 6.9 | 6.2 | 11.7 | 16.9 | 51.7 | 6.0 |
| 4. Great differences in wealth or income are unfair | 1.3 | 21.7 | 9.2 | 15.7 | 15.9 | 32.9 | 3.3 |
| 5. People who create wealth and jobs should be more highly rewarded than those who don't | 1.1 | 11.5 | 3.7 | 14.5 | 17.9 | 46.8 | 4.5 |

**C8** In Ireland today people have different views about what is fair and unfair in the way social services are provided. I would like you to tell me how much you Disagree or Agree with the following statements. [Int Show Card C1 and tick (✓) one box on each line].

*It is fair that:*

| | Strongly Disagree | Disagree | Slightly Disagree | Neither Agree nor Disagree | Slightly Agree | Agree | Strongly Agree |
|---|---|---|---|---|---|---|---|
| 1. people with private health insurance (like VHI and BUPA) can get better access to hospitals and consultants | 6.3 | 28.1 | 5.8 | 4.4 | 11.4 | 37.4 | 6.5 |
| 2. people with more money can afford to get a better education for their children | 5.1 | 28.8 | 7.2 | 4.4 | 9.2 | 38.4 | 6.9 |
| 3. people with higher incomes can buy extra pension provision for their retirement | 1.5 | 11.7 | 4.8 | 5.4 | 10.2 | 57.6 | 8.7 |
| 4. when new homes are being built, private housing and Corporation/Council housing are kept in separate estates | 3.3 | 24.5 | 8.5 | 14.6 | 9.6 | 36.0 | 3.5 |

**C9** People have different views about how much responsibility the family should take and how much the government should take for providing certain services. I would like you to consider 4 areas of life and would ask you to say how much responsibility you think the family or the government should take in each. For each of the 4 areas shown on this card please choose a point on the scale that indicates how you think provision should be made – by families, by the government, or somewhere in between. [Int. Show Card C4]

1. *a. Cost of Childcare for working parents*

Parents or family should take full responsibility →→→ The government should take full responsibility

| 0 | 1 | 2 | 3 | 4 | 5 | 6 | 7 | 8 | 9 | 10 |
|---|---|---|---|---|---|---|---|---|---|---|
| 9.3 | 6.2 | 5.2 | 5.4 | 8.8 | 35.3 | 9.1 | 7.5 | 7.2 | 2.5 | 3.6 |

2. *b. Cost of Help for Elderly People Living Alone in the community*

Parents or family should take full responsibility →→→ The government should take full responsibility

| 0 | 1 | 2 | 3 | 4 | 5 | 6 | 7 | 8 | 9 | 10 |
|---|---|---|---|---|---|---|---|---|---|---|
| 0.9 | 0.9 | 1.0 | 2.2 | 2.7 | 23.0 | 7.8 | 11.1 | 19.3 | 9.3 | 22.0 |

3. *c. Cost of Nursing home care for older people*

Parents or family should take full responsibility →→→ The government should take full responsibility

| 0 | 1 | 2 | 3 | 4 | 5 | 6 | 7 | 8 | 9 | 10 |
|---|---|---|---|---|---|---|---|---|---|---|
| 0.3 | 0.6 | 1.1 | 1.6 | 2.9 | 25.8 | 8.1 | 12.8 | 14.2 | 10.0 | 22.5 |

4. *d. Cost of Financial Support for Carers*

Parents or family should take full responsibility →→→ The government should take full responsibility

| 0 | 1 | 2 | 3 | 4 | 5 | 6 | 7 | 8 | 9 | 10 |
|---|---|---|---|---|---|---|---|---|---|---|
| 0.2 | 0.4 | 0.5 | 0.9 | 2.3 | 20.2 | 8.3 | 12.2 | 15.9 | 10.2 | 29.0 |

**C10**    **Interviewer Record Time (24 hour clock)**

# SECTION D   MINORITY GROUPS

**D1**   In general terms, how close do you feel to a) your neighbourhood/community; b) your town/city; c) your county; d)Ireland, e) Europe? [Int. Show Card D1]

|  | Very Close | Close | Not Very Close | Not Close At All | Can't Choose |
|---|---|---|---|---|---|
| a) your neighbourhood/community | 29.9 | 45.2 | 18.5 | 5.2 | 1.2 |
| b) your town/city | 16.3 | 52.2 | 24.8 | 5.1 | 1.5 |
| c) your county | 17.5 | 52.3 | 22.8 | 5.5 | 1.9 |
| d) Ireland | 27.9 | 53.6 | 13.5 | 3.1 | 1.9 |
| e) Europe | 5.9 | 31.3 | 41.3 | 18.6 | 2.9 |

**D2**   Would you say you are very proud, quite proud, not very proud, not at all proud to be Irish?

| Very proud | Quite proud | Not very proud | Not at all proud | Not applicable |
|---|---|---|---|---|
| 55.8 | 38.2 | 3.1 | 0.8 | 2.2 |

**D3**   Some people say the following things are important for being truly Irish. Others say they are not important. How important do you think each of the following is? [Int. Please tick (✓) one box on each line]

For being truly Irish, how important is it:

|  | Very Important | Fairly important | Not very important | Not important at all | Can't choose |
|---|---|---|---|---|---|
| 1. to have been born in Ireland | 49.2 | 29.2 | 14.2 | 6.0 | 1.4 |
| 2. to have Irish citizenship | 58.1 | 31.2 | 7.7 | 2.6 | 0.5 |
| 3. to have lived in Ireland for most of one's life | 42.3 | 36.2 | 16.4 | 4.7 | 0.4 |
| 4. to be able to speak Irish | 12.3 | 22.9 | 37.9 | 26.0 | 0.9 |
| 5. to be a Catholic | 22.4 | 17.5 | 29.0 | 30.2 | 0.9 |
| 6. to respect Ireland's political institutions and laws | 41.4 | 41.1 | 11.2 | 5.2 | 1.1 |
| 7. to feel Irish | 55.7 | 32.3 | 6.9 | 3.3 | 1.8 |

**D4** **How much do you agree or disagree with the following statements?**

| | Strongly Agree | Agree | Neither agree nor disagree | Disagree | Strongly Disagree |
|---|---|---|---|---|---|
| 1. It is impossible for people who do not share Irish customs and traditions to become fully Irish | 5.2 | 37.5 | 17.7 | 35.8 | 3.8 |
| 2. Ethnic minorities should be given government assistance to preserve their customs and traditions | 3.3 | 37.6 | 24.4 | 30.2 | 4.6 |

**D5** **Some people are disturbed by the opinions, customs and way of life of people different from themselves. Do you personally find the presence of people of: (1) another race, (2) another nationality disturbing in your daily life?** [Int. Show Card D2]

*1. ANOTHER RACE*

Disturbing ──────────→ Not disturbing at all

| 1 | 2 | 3 | 4 | 5 |
|---|---|---|---|---|
| 3.7 | 4.8 | 12.1 | 15.5 | 63.8 |

*2. ANOTHER NATIONALITY*

Disturbing ──────────→ Not disturbing at all

| 1 | 2 | 3 | 4 | 5 |
|---|---|---|---|---|
| 3.5 | 3.0 | 11.4 | 15.3 | 66.8 |

**D6** **How much do you agree or disagree that refugees who have suffered political repression in their own country should be allowed to stay in Ireland?**

| Strongly agree | Agree | Neither agree nor disagree | Disagree | Strongly disagree |
|---|---|---|---|---|
| 16.3 | 51.2 | 21.0 | 9.3 | 2.2 |

**D7** Generally speaking how do you feel about the number of people: 1) of another race, 2) of another nationality, 3) of another culture living in our country: Are there, Too many, A lot but not too many, Not many?

| | Too many | A lot but not too many | Not many |
|---|---|---|---|
| 1) another race | 20.0 | 56.7 | 23.3 |
| 2) another nationality | 25.3 | 52.7 | 22.0 |
| 3) another culture | 20.7 | 52.4 | 26.9 |

**D8** People have different views about certain groups in society. I am going to read out a list of groups and I would like you to tell me how close you would allow members of each group. For each group I would like you to tell me whether or not you would be willing to: a) marry or welcome as members of your family; b) have as close friends; c) have as a next-door neighbour; d) work in the same work-place; e) welcome as Irish citizens; f) have as visitors only; g) debar or deport from Ireland. The main idea here is to get your first reaction, therefore, it would be better if we went through the list fairly quickly. [Int. Show Card D3 and tick (✓) one box on each row.]

| I would: | (a) Marry or welcome as members of my family | (b) Have as close friends | (c) Have as a next-door neighbour | (d) Work in the same work-place | (e) Welcome as Irish citizens | (f) Have as visitors only | (g) Debar or deport from Ireland |
|---|---|---|---|---|---|---|---|
| 1. English | 64.4 | 15.3 | 7.5 | 5.2 | 2.8 | 3.9 | 1.0 |
| 2. Jews | 30.2 | 20.3 | 14.5 | 10.3 | 7.4 | 14.1 | 3.4 |
| 3. Spaniards | 37.7 | 17.5 | 12.3 | 8.9 | 6.2 | 13.9 | 3.5 |
| 4. Travellers | 9.9 | 9.2 | 10.1 | 20.1 | 20.9 | 19.9 | 9.9 |
| 5. Romanians | 14.9 | 11.6 | 11.1 | 15.7 | 11.7 | 24.0 | 11.1 |
| 6. Indians (South Asians) | 16.4 | 13.4 | 11.8 | 14.8 | 11.1 | 25.0 | 7.5 |
| 7. Muslims | 12.4 | 13.8 | 11.7 | 13.4 | 9.7 | 28.0 | 10.9 |
| 8. Nigerians | 15.0 | 12.8 | 10.9 | 14.4 | 10.7 | 26.3 | 9.9 |
| 9. Protestants | 48.4 | 20.1 | 10.7 | 6.2 | 5.8 | 6.7 | 2.1 |
| 10. Bosnians | 17.5 | 12.2 | 13.8 | 16.2 | 10.1 | 23.1 | 7.2 |
| 11. Chinese | 19.1 | 14.7 | 14.6 | 16.0 | 10.4 | 20.5 | 4.8 |
| 12. Arabs | 13.0 | 12.4 | 11.0 | 14.9 | 8.0 | 30.6 | 10.1 |
| 13. Black Americans | 21.2 | 15.9 | 11.4 | 14.7 | 9.3 | 20.5 | 7.0 |

**D9a** **Some people say that it is better for a country if different racial and ethnic groups maintain their distinct customs and traditions. Others say it is better if these groups adapt and blend into the larger society in Ireland. Which of these views comes closer to your own?** [Int. Please tick (✓) one box only.]

1. Better for a country if different racial and ethnic groups maintain their distinct customs and traditions    40.1
2. Others say it is better if these groups adapt & blend into the larger society in Ireland    59.9

**D9b** **When answering this question which group (or groups) had you in mind?**

**D10** **Thinking again about different racial and ethnic minority groups, please tell me whether you tend to Agree or tend to Disagree with the following statements?**

|  | Tend to Agree | Tend to Disagree | DK |
|---|---|---|---|
| 1. In schools where there are too many children from these minority groups, the quality of education suffers | 39.5 | 40.1 | 20.4 |
| 2. People from these minority groups abuse the system of social benefits | 53.7 | 27.5 | 18.7 |
| 3. The authorities should make efforts to improve the situation of people from these minority groups | 65.2 | 21.6 | 13.1 |
| 4. People from these minority groups are enriching the cultural life of Ireland | 42.4 | 39.5 | 18.1 |
| 5. The religious practices of people from these minority groups threaten our way of life | 13.8 | 75.1 | 11.1 |
| 6. The presence of people from these minority groups increases unemployment in Ireland | 49.0 | 39.9 | 11.1 |
| 7. Discrimination in the job market on grounds of a person's race, religion or culture should be outlawed. | 79.6 | 12.4 | 7.9 |
| 8. Minority groups have an unfair advantage in getting Local Authority housing | 39.8 | 31.7 | 28.6 |

**D11** [Int. Show Card D4] **The ladders below represent the distribution of economic wealth (money *and* property) in Ireland. Indicate, by placing an X in the ladder, how well YOU think each group is doing relative to the richest and poorest people in Ireland. So, for example, if you believe that some group is doing only slightly better than the very poorest people in the country you would respond by placing the X close to the bottom rung of the ladder.**

For example:

(1) the wealthiest people in Ireland would be represented like this …

**1   RICHEST**

☐6
☐5
☐4
☐3
☐2
☐1

**POOREST**

(2) the least well-off would be represented like this …

**2   RICHEST**

☐6
☐5
☐4
☐3
☐2
☐1

**POOREST**

Now place an X on a rung of the ladder, that best represents in your opinion, the wealth of the following four groups in Ireland … [Int. Tick (✓) one box in columns (1), (2), (3), (4)]

| (1) The average income of the Travelling community | (2) Families in inner city Dublin | (3) Romanian asylum-seeker in Ireland | (4) Your own household |
|---|---|---|---|
| **RICHEST** | **RICHEST** | **RICHEST** | **RICHEST** |
| 5.7 | 0.8 | 1.1 | 3.0 |
| 11.9 | 2.4 | 2.9 | 17.1 |
| 25.9 | 10.2 | 7.2 | 49.4 |
| 25.5 | 27.2 | 20.0 | 24.7 |
| 18.7 | 34.5 | 33.3 | 4.3 |
| 12.2 | 24.8 | 35.6 | 1.5 |
| **POOREST** | **POOREST** | **POOREST** | **POOREST** |

**D12** **From this list, I would like you to tell me if there are: (a) many such people; (b) Some; or (c) none who live: (1) in your neighbourhood: (2) who are among your friends and (3) who work with you?** [Int. Show Card D5 and tick (✓) one box on each row]

| | Many | Some | None | N/A |
|---|---|---|---|---|
| 1. In the neighbourhood | | | | |
| a. Persons of another nationality | 7.6 | 59.4 | 33.1 | |
| b. Persons of another race | 6.4 | 49.2 | 44.4 | |
| c. Persons of another culture | 6.9 | 52.7 | 40.4 | |
| 2. Among your friends | | | | |
| a. Persons of another nationality | 7.1 | 45.5 | 47.4 | |
| b. Persons of another race | 2.7 | 29.3 | 68.0 | |
| c. Persons of another culture | 3.6 | 32.5 | 64.0 | |
| 3. At work with you | | | | |
| a. Persons of another nationality | 6.1 | 28.7 | 35.0 | 30.2 |
| b. Persons of another race | 4.5 | 20.9 | 43.8 | 30.7 |
| c. Persons of another culture | 4.9 | 22.5 | 41.7 | 30.9 |

**D13** **Please indicate how closely you Agree or Disagree with the following statements.** [Int: Tick (✓) one box on each row]

| | Strongly Agree | Agree | Neither Agree nor Disagree | Disagree | Strongly Disagree |
|---|---|---|---|---|---|
| 1. At times I think I am no good at all. | 2.0 | 19.1 | 11.6 | 44.7 | 22.7 |
| 2. I feel that I have a number of good qualities. | 22.5 | 72.8 | 2.9 | 0.9 | 0.9 |
| 3. I certainly feel useless at times. | 2.4 | 30.2 | 11.1 | 38.2 | 18.1 |
| 4. I take a positive attitude towards myself. | 22.8 | 61.8 | 10.6 | 3.8 | 0.9 |

**D14** Some people say that they are not at all racist. Others feel that they are very racist. Would you look at this card [Int: Show Card D6.] and give me the number that shows your own feelings about this? If you feel you are not at all racist, you give a score of 1. If you feel you are very racist, you give a score of 10. The scores between 1 and 10 allow you to say how close to either side you are.

NOT RACIST AT ALL ⟶ VERY RACIST

| 1 | 2 | 3 | 4 | 5 | 6 | 7 | 8 | 9 | 10 |
|---|---|---|---|---|---|---|---|---|----|
| 31.8 | 21.6 | 14.2 | 8.0 | 12.1 | 4.1 | 3.7 | 2.2 | 1.2 | 1.2 |

**D15** Interviewer Record Time (24 hour clock)

# SECTION E   THE ENVIRONMENT

**E1** How much do you agree or disagree with each of the following two statements? [Int. Show Card E1 and tick (✓) one box on each line]

|  | Strongly Agree | Agree | Neither agree nor disagree | Disagree | Strongly Disagree | Can't choose |
|---|---|---|---|---|---|---|
| 1. Private enterprise is the best way to solve Ireland's economic problems | 7.0 | 37.2 | 26.9 | 16.3 | 3.2 | 9.5 |
| 2. It is the responsibility of the government to reduce the differences in income between people with high incomes and those with low incomes | 10.0 | 53.8 | 15.5 | 15.8 | 1.3 | 3.6 |

**E2** Looking at the items on this card [Int. Show Card E2] please indicate what you think should be (1) Ireland's highest priority and (2) Ireland's second highest priority – the second most important thing it should do?

| | Maintain order in the nation | Give people more say in government decisions | Fight rising prices | Protect freedom of speech | Can't choose |
|---|---|---|---|---|---|
| (1) **Highest priority** | 45.9 | 22.4 | 16.4 | 9.5 | 5.8 |
| (2) **Second priority** | 19.4 | 25.8 | 26.3 | 22.3 | 6.1 |

**E3** **How much do you agree or disagree with each of the following statements?** [Int: Show Card E1 and tick (✓) one box on each line]

| | Strongly Agree | Agree | Neither agree nor disagree | Disagree | Strongly Disagree | Can't choose |
|---|---|---|---|---|---|---|
| 1. We believe too often in science, and not enough in feelings and faith | 6.2 | 43.8 | 20.2 | 21.7 | 2.0 | 6.1 |
| 2. Overall, modern science does more harm than good | 2.0 | 17.5 | 15.4 | 54.2 | 5.3 | 5.5 |
| 3. Modern science will solve our environmental problems with little change to our way of life | 0.7 | 20.3 | 21.0 | 44.4 | 5.3 | 8.3 |
| 4. We worry too much about the future of the environment and not enough about prices and jobs today | 3.6 | 23.0 | 14.4 | 48.7 | 7.1 | 3.1 |
| 5. Almost everything we do in modern life harms the environment | 4.1 | 46.4 | 15.5 | 29.5 | 1.6 | 3.0 |
| 6. People worry too much about human progress harming the environment | 0.6 | 28.2 | 14.8 | 47.3 | 4.7 | 4.5 |
| 7. In order to protect the environment Ireland needs economic growth | 2.5 | 44.0 | 17.0 | 28.1 | 1.8 | 6.7 |

| | Strongly Agree | Agree | Neither agree nor disagree | Disagree | Strongly Disagree | Can't choose |
|---|---|---|---|---|---|---|
| 8. It is right to use animals for medical testing if it might save human lives | 5.7 | 48.6 | 12.6 | 20.0 | 7.9 | 5.1 |
| 9. Economic growth always harms the environment | 1.1 | 20.0 | 21.1 | 49.3 | 2.2 | 6.3 |
| 10. The earth simply cannot continue to support population growth at its present rate | 4.7 | 40.3 | 18.7 | 23.5 | 1.2 | 11.7 |

**E4   Please tick one box to show which statement is closest to your views.** [Int. Show Card E3 and tick (✓) one box only]

| | |
|---|---|
| Nature is sacred because it is created by God | 38.2 |
| Nature is spiritual or sacred in itself | 23.3 |
| Nature is important, but not spiritual or sacred | 27.3 |
| Can't choose | 11.2 |

**E5   How willing would you be:** [Int: Please tick (✓) one box on each line]

| | Very Willing | Fairly willing | Neither willing nor unwilling | Fairly unwilling | Very unwilling | Can't choose |
|---|---|---|---|---|---|---|
| 1. to pay much higher prices in order to protect the environment? | 6.1 | 45.2 | 14.3 | 19.6 | 10.6 | 4.2 |
| 2. to pay much higher taxes in order to protect the environment? | 4.1 | 29.3 | 14.0 | 29.0 | 18.8 | 4.8 |
| 3. to accept cuts in your standard of living in order to protect the environment? | 4.4 | 30.4 | 16.9 | 26.5 | 18.2 | 3.6 |

**E6** How much do you agree or disagree with each of these statements? [Int: Show Card E1 and tick (✓) one box on each line]

| | Strongly Agree | Agree | Neither agree nor disagree | Disagree | Strongly Disagree | Can't choose |
|---|---|---|---|---|---|---|
| 1. It is just too difficult for someone like me to do much about the environment | 2.6 | 28.8 | 7.2 | 52.5 | 5.7 | 3.1 |
| 2. I do what is right for the environment, even when it costs more money or takes more time | 2.9 | 49.7 | 19.6 | 23.2 | 1.2 | 3.4 |
| 3. There are more important things to do in life than protect the environment | 2.1 | 23.0 | 17.7 | 48.0 | 6.5 | 2.8 |
| 4. There is no point in doing what I can for the environment unless others do the same | 4.5 | 42.0 | 6.0 | 42.3 | 3.5 | 1.6 |
| 5. Many of the claims about environmental threats are exaggerated | 1.7 | 23.4 | 15.9 | 45.1 | 7.7 | 6.2 |

**E7** I am going to read out 6 statements. I would like you to tell me how true you think each is. [Int: Please tick (✓) one box on each line – show card E4]

| | Definitely true | Probably true | Probably not true | Definitely not true | Can't choose |
|---|---|---|---|---|---|
| In your opinion, how true is this? | | | | | |
| 1. 'Antibiotics can kill bacteria but not viruses' | 29.9 | 39.7 | 7.0 | 4.7 | 18.7 |
| 2. 'Human beings developed from earlier species of animals' | 23.7 | 40.4 | 11.1 | 12.4 | 12.4 |
| 3. 'All man-made chemicals can cause cancer if you eat enough of them' | 13.0 | 41.5 | 19.4 | 12.1 | 14.0 |
| 4. 'If someone is exposed to any amount of radioactivity they are certain to die as a result' | 12.0 | 31.8 | 25.4 | 20.6 | 10.3 |
| 5. 'The greenhouse effect (global warming) is caused by a hole in the earth's atmosphere' | 36.4 | 44.6 | 4.2 | 5.9 | 8.9 |

| | Definitely true | Probably true | Probably not true | Definitely not true | Can't choose |
|---|---|---|---|---|---|
| 6. 'Every time we use coal or oil or gas, we contribute to the greenhouse effect' (global warming) | 36.6 | 44.6 | 7.0 | 2.6 | 9.2 |

**E8a** In general, how dangerous do you think that air pollution caused by cars is on the environment? [Int: Show Card E5 and tick (✓) one box only]

| extremely dangerous for the environment | very dangerous | somewhat dangerous | not very dangerous | not dangerous at all for the environment | Can't choose |
|---|---|---|---|---|---|
| 15.2 | 35.7 | 39.6 | 6.0 | 0.6 | 2.9 |

**E8b** And how dangerous do you think that air pollution caused by cars is to you and your family? [Int: Show Card E6 and tick (✓) one box only]

| extremely dangerous for you and your family | very dangerous | somewhat dangerous | not very dangerous | not dangerous at all for you and your family | Can't choose |
|---|---|---|---|---|---|
| 6.9 | 21.3 | 47.7 | 18.4 | 2.7 | 2.8 |

**E9a** In general, do you think that air pollution caused by industry is ... [Int: Show Card E5 and tick (✓) one box only]

| extremely dangerous for the environment | very dangerous | somewhat dangerous | not very dangerous | not dangerous at all for the environment | Can't choose |
|---|---|---|---|---|---|
| 19.1 | 40.0 | 34.0 | 4.1 | 0.1 | 2.7 |

**E9b** And do you think that pesticides and chemicals used in farming are: ... [Int: Show Card E5 and tick (✓) one box only]

| extremely dangerous for the environment | very dangerous | somewhat dangerous | not very dangerous | not dangerous at all for the environment | Can't choose |
|---|---|---|---|---|---|
| 14.8 | 35.5 | 40.1 | 6.1 | 0.6 | 2.8 |

**E9c**  And do you think that pollution of Ireland's rivers, lakes and streams is … [Int: Show Card E5 and tick (✓) one box only]

| extremely dangerous for the environment | very dangerous | somewhat dangerous | not very dangerous | not dangerous at all for the environment | Can't choose |
|---|---|---|---|---|---|
| 23.3 | 40.2 | 30.1 | 3.8 | 0.3 | 2.4 |

**E10a**  In general, do you think that a rise in the world's temperature caused by the 'greenhouse effect' (global warming) is … [Int: Show Card E5 and tick (✓) one box only]

| extremely dangerous for the environment | very dangerous | somewhat dangerous | not very dangerous | not dangerous at all for the environment | Can't choose |
|---|---|---|---|---|---|
| 19.3 | 32.9 | 34.8 | 5.9 | 0.5 | 6.6 |

**E10b**  And do you think that modifying the genes of certain crops is … [Int: Show Card E5 and tick (✓) one box only]

| extremely dangerous for the environment | very dangerous | somewhat dangerous | not very dangerous | not dangerous at all for the environment | Can't choose |
|---|---|---|---|---|---|
| 15.2 | 25.7 | 34.5 | 10.4 | 1.3 | 12.9 |

**E11a**  If you had to choose, which one of the following would be closest to your views? [Int: Show Card E7 and tick (✓) one box only]

| Government should let ordinary people decide for themselves how to protect the environment, even if it means they don't always do the right thing | 17.3 |
|---|---|

OR

| Government should pass laws to make ordinary people protect the environment, even if it interferes with people's rights to make their own decisions | 71.3 |
|---|---|
| Can't choose | 11.4 |

**E11b  And which one of the following would be closest to your views?** [Int: Show Card E8 and tick (✓) one box only]

Government should let businesses decide for themselves how to protect the environment, even if it means they don't always do the right thing   6.3

OR

Government should pass laws to make businesses protect the environment, even if it interferes with businesses' rights to make their own decisions   85.7

Can't choose   8.0

**E12  Some countries are doing more to protect the world environment than other countries are. In general, do you think that Ireland is doing …** [Int: Please tick (✓) one box only]

More than enough   2.1     About the right amount   32.1     Too little   56.9     Can't choose   8.9

**E13a  On balance, which of these two do you think is making more effort to look after the environment** [Int: Please tick (✓) one box only]

Business and industry   10.9     People in general   51.6     Both equally   21.9     Can't choose   15.6

**E13b  And which of these two groups do you think is making more effort to look after the environment…** [Int: Please tick (✓) one box only]

Government   41.8     Business and industy   9.6     Both equally   26.4     Can't choose   22.1

**E13c  And which of these two groups is making more effort to look after the environment…** [Int: Please tick (✓) one box only]

People in general   37.0     Government   21.4     Both equally   25.8     Can't choose   15.8

**E14** **How much do you agree or disagree with each of these statements?** [Int: Show Card E9 and tick (✓) one box on each line]

|  | Strongly Agree | Agree | Neither agree nor disagree | Disagree | Strongly Disagree | Can't choose |
|---|---|---|---|---|---|---|
| 1. For environmental problems, there should be international agreements that Ireland and other countries should be made to follow | 22.4 | 61.2 | 6.6 | 4.7 | 0.1 | 5.0 |
| 2. Poorer countries should be expected to make less effort than richer countries to protect the environment | 2.6 | 27.0 | 11.2 | 47.9 | 6.7 | 4.6 |
| 3. Economic progress in Ireland will slow down unless we look after the environment better | 6.5 | 43.2 | 20.2 | 19.8 | 1.0 | 9.3 |

**E15** **How likely do you think that, within the next five years, an accident at a nuclear power station will cause long-term environmental damage across many countries?** [Int: Please tick (✓) one box only]

Very likely 21.3    Likely 44.9    Unlikely 19.8    Very Unlikely 5.3    Can't choose 8.8

**E16** **How much trust do you have in each of the following groups to give you correct information about causes of pollution?** [Int: Show Card E10 and please tick (✓) one box on each line]

|  | A great deal of trust | Quite a lot of trust | Some trust | Not much trust | Hardly any trust | Can't choose |
|---|---|---|---|---|---|---|
| 1. Business and industry | 1.4 | 5.8 | 36.2 | 33.8 | 19.2 | 3.7 |
| 2. Environmental groups | 20.5 | 41.8 | 27.7 | 4.9 | 2.1 | 3.0 |
| 3. Government departments | 2.9 | 22.1 | 45.4 | 19.3 | 7.2 | 3.0 |
| 4. Newspapers | 4.3 | 19.9 | 44.8 | 19.6 | 8.6 | 2.8 |
| 5. Radio or TV programmes | 6.6 | 32.3 | 46.4 | 9.0 | 3.1 | 2.6 |
| 6. University research centres | 27.9 | 42.4 | 21.7 | 3.1 | 1.3 | 3.5 |

**E17a** **How often do you make a special effort to sort glass or tins or plastic or newspapers and so on for recycling?** [Int: Please tick (✓) one box only]

Always  25.3    Often  21.9    Sometimes  26.7    Never  18.0    Recycling not available where I live  8.2

**E17b.** **And how often do you cut back on driving a car for environmental reasons?** [Int: Please tick (✓) one box only]

Always  1.9    Often  5.9    Sometimes  16.8    Never  51.4    I do not have or cannot drive a car  24.0

**E18** **Are you a member of any group whose main aim is to preserve or protect the environment?** [Int: Please tick (✓) one box only]

YES  3.9      NO  96.1

**E19** **In the last five years, have you …** [Int: Please tick (✓) one box on each line]

|  | Yes I have | No I have not |
|---|---|---|
| 1. signed a petition about an environmental issue? | 26.4 | 73.6 |
| 2. given money to an environmental group? | 20.4 | 79.6 |
| 3. taken part in a protest or demonstration about an environmental issue? | 4.6 | 95.4 |

**E20** **Please tick one box below to show which statement comes closest to expressing what you believe about God** [Int: Show Card E11 and tick (✓) one box only]

| | |
|---|---|
| 1. I don't believe in God | 2.9 |
| 2. I don't know whether there is a God and I don't believe there is any way to find out | 4.6 |
| 3. I don't believe in a personal God, but I do believe in a Higher Power of some kind | 8.3 |
| 4. I find myself believing in God some of the time but not at others | 10.6 |
| 5. While I have doubts, I feel that I do believe in God | 26.7 |
| 6. I know God really exists and I have no doubts about it | 44.5 |
| 7. Can't choose | 2.4 |

**E21** Would you describe the place where you live as … [Int: Please tick (✓) one box only]

| A big city | the suburbs or outskirts of a big city | a small city or town | a country village | a farm or home in the country |
|---|---|---|---|---|
| 6.2 | 27.9 | 27.3 | 9.4 | 29.3 |

**E22** In general, do you think that nuclear power stations are … [Int: Show Card E5 and please tick (✓) one box only]

| extremely dangerous for the environment | very dangerous | somewhat dangerous | not very dangerous | not dangerous at all for the environment | Can't choose |
|---|---|---|---|---|---|
| 47.1 | 31.6 | 17.6 | 1.5 | 0.3 | 1.8 |

**E23** How much do you agree or disagree with each of these statements? [Int: Please tick (✓) one box on each line]

| | Strongly Agree | Agree | Neither agree nor disagree | Disagree | Strongly Disagree | Can't choose |
|---|---|---|---|---|---|---|
| 1. Government should redistribute income from the better-off to those who are less well off | 8.5 | 43.1 | 15.8 | 27.1 | 2.6 | 2.9 |
| 2. There is little that people can do to change the course of their lives | 1.4 | 14.2 | 7.1 | 62.4 | 13.7 | 1.3 |
| 3. One of the problems with people today is that they challenge authority too often | 2.9 | 27.7 | 15.5 | 44.4 | 6.7 | 2.9 |
| 4. People with money should be left to enjoy it | 5.5 | 64.4 | 18.3 | 8.2 | 1.2 | 2.5 |
| 5. There are times when people should follow their consciences even if it means breaking the law | 2.9 | 32.2 | 16.1 | 37.5 | 5.7 | 5.5 |
| 6. Private enterprise needs to be controlled to protect everyone's needs | 4.2 | 54.0 | 19.0 | 13.5 | 1.7 | 7.6 |
| 7. All societies have inequalities which it is better not to interfere with | 1.1 | 24.6 | 21.7 | 38.2 | 3.6 | 10.8 |

|  | Strongly Agree | Agree | Neither agree nor disagree | Disagree | Strongly Disagree | Can't choose |
|---|---|---|---|---|---|---|
| 8. Taking everything into account, the world is getting better | 2.3 | 42.4 | 19.1 | 27.7 | 4.3 | 4.3 |

**E24  Interviewer Record Time (24 hour clock)** ☐☐☐☐

# SECTION F  SOCIO-DEMOGRAPHICS

**F1  Sex of respondent**    Male **49.2**    Female **50.8**

**F2  Could I ask for your date of birth**    Day ☐☐    Month ☐☐    Year ☐☐☐☐

**F3a  Could I ask about your current marital status? Are you:**

| Married | Separated | Divorced | Widowed | Never married |
|---|---|---|---|---|
| **49.3** | **2.6** | **0.7** | **6.5** | **40.9** |

**F3b  Are you currently living with your husband/wife?**

Yes **97.7**    No **2.3**

**F3c  Are you currently living with another partner?**    Yes **83.1**    No **16.9**

**F3d  Are you currently living with a partner?**    Yes **9.8**    No **90.2**

**F4a  How many years of full-time education did you receive?** [Int: If respondent did not return to full-time education as an adult calculate as (age when left full-time education minus 5)]

_____ years of full-time education          No formal education ☐₁

**F4b**  **Which of the following best describes the highest level of education you have completed to date.** [Int. Please tick (✓) one box only]

| | |
|---|---|
| None | 1.0 |
| Incomplete Primary | 2.5 |
| Complete Primary | 11.8 |
| Started Second Level but no exams taken | 7.0 |
| Group Cert or equivalent | 5.3 |
| Junior/Intermediate Cert or equivalent | 14.8 |
| Leaving Cert or equiv. | 23.7 |
| Started Third Level but did not complete | 3.5 |
| Certificate or diploma | 14.4 |
| University primary degree or equivalent | 9.4 |
| University higher degree or equivalent | 6.7 |

**F5**  **During the last five years have you been unemployed and seeking work? By unemployed I mean available for and actively seeking work in contrast, for example, to someone who is engaged in home duties.**

Yes   12.7 → go to F6          No   87.3 → go to F7

**F6**  **For how many months, over the last five years were you unemployed?** _____

**F7**  **Which of the following best describes your present situation with regard to employment:** [Int. Please tick (✓) one box only]

| | | |
|---|---|---|
| At work full-time (30 hrs or more) | 45.1 → | **Go to F9** |
| At work part-time (less than 30 hrs weekly) | 10.0 → | **Go to F9** |
| At work as relative assisting/unpaid family worker | 0.9 → | **Go to F9** |
| Unemployed and seeking work | 3.3 → | **Go to F8** |
| Student | 10.6 → | **Go to F8** |
| Retired | 8.7 → | **Go to F8** |
| Engaged in home duties | 18.6 → | **Go to F8** |
| Long term sick or disabled | 1.9 → | **Go to F8** |
| Other, specify _____ | 0.8 → | **Go to F8** |

**F8** [Int: For people who are unemployed or coded 4-9 in question F7] **Did you ever work at any time in the past, even if not currently working now?**

Yes    78.2          No      21.8 → go to F14

**F8b**    **When did you give up this job?** _____ month _____ year → go to F9

**F9**    **How many hours do/did you normally work per week–including usual overtime if any?** _____ hours

**F10a**   **What is/was your occupation? Please describe fully. If farmer please record the number of acres farmed. If appropriate, please record the rank or grade, e.g. Civil Service, Gardai, Defence Forces etc.**

_____

_____

**F10b**   **Please describe as fully as possible the nature of the business activity of your employer.**

_____

_____

**F11a**   **Do/did you work in the public or private sector?** [PLEASE TICK ONE BOX ONLY]

| | |
|---|---|
| Civil Service | 7.7 |
| Local Authority Health Board or VEC | 9.4 |
| Non-commercial semi-state body | 1.3 |
| Semi-state body | 6.8 |
| Private sector | 74.8 |

**F11b  Are/were you self employed (including farmer) or are you an employee?**

Self employed    16.1          Employee    83.9

    **F11c  How many people do/did you employ, including yourself?** _____

**F11d  Are/were you a member of any trade union at this time?**    Yes    33.6    No    66.4

**F11e  Do you normally supervise any other workers in your job?**

Yes    33.1                    No                    66.9 → **Go to F12**

    **F11f  Approximately how many do you supervise?** _____    → **Go to F13**

**F12  How worried are you that you might become unemployed in the next year?**

Very worried   3.6        Somewhat worried   6.9        A little worried   12.3        Not at all worried   77.2

**F13  If you did become unemployed how long do you think it would take you to find a suitable job?** _____

**F14  [Int: check marital status at question F3] Is the respondent married or living with a partner?**

    Yes    55.7 → go to F15          No    44.3 → go to F19

**F15  In relation to employment could you describe your spouse's /partner's situation at present?** [Int. Please tick (✓) one box only]

| | | |
|---|---|---|
| At work full-time (30 hrs or more) | 51.5 → **Go to F18** | Student | 0.5 → **Go to F16** |
| At work part-time (less than 30 hrs weekly) | 14.6 → **Go to F18** | Retired | 10.3 → **Go to F16** |
| At work as relative assisting/unpaid family worker | 0.4 → **Go to F18** | Engaged in home duties | 17.2 → **Go to F16** |
| Unemployed and seeking work | 2.0 → **Go to F16** | Long term sick and disabled | 2.5 → **Go to F16** |
| | | Other, specify _____ | 0.9 → **Go to F16** |

**F16** [Int: For people whose spouse/partner are unemployed or coded 4–9 in question F15 above] **Did your spouse ever work at any time in the past, even if not currently working now?**

Yes  81.9     No     18.1 → go to F19

**F17  When did she/he give up this job?** _____ month _____ year → go to F18

**F18**  **What is/was your spouse's occupation? Please describe as fully as possible. If farmer please record the number of acres farmed. If appropriate, please record the rank or grade, e.g. Civil Service, Gardai, Defence Forces etc**

_____

_____

**F19**  **When you were 16 what kind of work did your father do– what was his occupation? Please describe fully. If farmer please record number of acres farmed. If appropriate, please record the rank or grade, e.g. Civil Service, Gardai, Defence Forces etc**

_____

_____

**F20**  **What were some of your father's main duties at work? Please write in a description of his duties.**

_____

_____

**F21**  **With regard to your accommodation, could you tell me if it is…. Int. Please tick (→) one box only]**

A house or a flat that you are buying on a mortgage                                      29.3

A house or a flat that you are purchasing under a local authority tenant purchase scheme   3.1

A house or a flat that you own outright                                                  40.6

A house or a flat that you are renting from the local authority                           5.9

A house or a flat that you are renting privately                                          7.0

Other, please specify                                                                    14.0

_____

**F22** **Do you belong to any religious denomination?**
Yes   87.8 → Which one?        No   11.8 → go to F23        Don't Know   0.5 → go to F23

**F23** **Did your family belong to any religion when you were 16 years of age? Please describe as fully as possible.** [Int: If none, write NONE, DO NOT LEAVE BLANK]

_____

## IF RELIGION GIVEN AT EITHER F22 OR F23 ABOVE

**F24** **How often nowadays do you attend religious services?** [Int: Show Card F1 and tick (✓) one box only]

| | |
|---|---|
| Several times a week | 9.9 |
| Once a week | 46.7 |
| 2 or 3 times a month | 7.8 |
| Once a month | 5.0 |
| Several times a year | 13.9 |
| Once a year | 6.7 |
| Less Frequently | 4.2 |
| Never | 5.9 |

**F25** **Using this card can you tell me if you personally believe that God exists or not? People who believe that God definitely *does not* exist would give a score of '0'. People who fully believe that God definitely *does* exist, would give a score of '10'. Other people would place themselves somewhere in between these two views. Where would you place yourself on this scale?** [Int. Show Card F2 and tick (✓) one box on each line]

*God definitely*
*DOES NOT exist* ————————————————————→ *God definitely*
*DOES EXIST*

| 0 | 1 | 2 | 3 | 4 | 5 | 6 | 7 | 8 | 9 | 10 |
|---|---|---|---|---|---|---|---|---|---|---|
| 2.7 | 1.4 | 1.8 | 1.1 | 1.3 | 10.0 | 3.0 | 6.3 | 10.9 | 10.5 | 51.0 |

**F26** **For about how much time, if any, have you ever lived outside the Republic of Ireland, not counting periods of less than three months?** [Int. Please tick (✓) one box on each line]

| | |
|---|---|
| Never lived outside the Republic of Ireland for a period of three months or more | 70.0 |
| Lived for more than three months but less than a year | 6.5 |
| Lived for 1 to less than 2 years | 5.3 |
| Lived for 2 to less than 3 years | 3.4 |
| Lived for 3 to less than 4 years | 2.4 |
| 4 years or longer | 12.3 |

**F27** **Many people think of themselves as being part of a particular nationality, for example as French or American or whatever. Do you think of yourself as Irish or as belonging to some other nationality, or do you not think of yourself in this way?** [Int. Show Card F3 and tick (X) one box only]

*I think of myself as:*

| | | |
|---|---|---|
| Irish | 96.3 | → go to F28 |
| Another nationality | 1.4 → Which one? | → go to F28 |
| A combination of different nationalities | 1.3 → Which one's? | → go to F28 |
| I don't think of myself in this way | 1.0 | → go to F29 |

**F28** **Overall how important is it to you that you are 'Irish' [if code 1 at F27] or other nationality (ies) [read out nationality if code 2 or 3 at F27]?**

Very important   65.8      Fairly important   27.4      Not very important   6.0      Not important at all   0.9

**F29** **Are you a citizen of Ireland?**

Yes, citizen of Ireland   98.5          No   1.5

> **F30** **Which country are you a citizen of?** _____ (please specify) → **go to F31**

**F31** Can you tell me whether or not (1) your mother and (2) your father was a citizen of Ireland when you were born? [Int. Please tick (✓) one box only]

|  |  |  |  |
|---|---|---|---|
| (1) Mother | Yes | 95.9 | No | 4.1 |
| (2) Father | Yes | 96.4 | No | 3.6 |

**F32** Some people also think of themselves as belonging to a larger group that includes people from other countries, for example, as European, North American, African and so on. How about you? Do you think of yourself in this way?

Yes   35.5 → Which group? _____ go to F33       No   64.5 → go to F34

**F33** Overall, how important is it to you that you are (read out the 'larger group' specified above)?

Very important   17.2      Fairly important   53.1      Not very important   26.7      Not important at all   3.0

**F34a** I would like to ask about the approximate level of net household income? This means the total income, after tax, PRSI and other statutory deductions, of *all* members of the household. It includes all types of income: income from employment, social welfare payments, child benefit, rents, interest, pensions etc. We would just like to know into which of four broad groups the total income of your household falls. I'd like to assure you once again that all information you give me is entirely confidential [Int. Show Card F4 and tick (✓) one box below]

| *Per week* | *Per Month* | *Per Year* | | |
|---|---|---|---|---|
| A. Under £190 | Under £825 | Under £10,000 | 17.3 | → *Go to Q.A below, Show Card A* |
| B. £191 – £360 | £826 – £1570 | £10,001 – £19,000 | 25.6 | → *Go to Q.B below, Show Card B* |
| C. £361 – £570 | £1571 – £2475 | £19,001 – £30,000 | 28.9 | → *Go to Q.C below, Show Card C* |
| D. £571 or more | £2476 or more | £30,001 or more | 28.2 | → *Go to Q.D below, Show Card D* |

**F34b** [INT: Show Card A, B, C or D from the yellow cards as appropriate. Tick ONE Box only below]

**A** Would that be:
(per week) Under £85 □1 £86–£110 □2 £111–£150 □3 £151–£190 □4
(per month) Under £370 □1 £371–£475 □2 £476–£650 □3 £651–£825 □4
(per year) Under £4500 □1 £4501–£5700 □2 £5701–£8000 □3 £8001–£10000 □4

**B** Would that be:
(per week) £191–£220 □1 £221–£270 □2 £271–£320 □3 £321–£360 □4
(per month) £826–£950 □1 £951–£1150 □2 £1151–£1400 □3 £1401–£1570 □4
(per year) £10001–£11500 □1 £11501–£14000 □2 £14001–£16500 □3 £16501–£19000 □4

**C** Would that be:
(per week) £361–£400 □1 £401–£450 □2 £451–£500 □3 £501–570 □4
(per month) £1571–£1750 □1 £1751–£2000 □2 £2001–£2200 □3 £2201–£2475 □4
(per year) £19001–£21000 □1 £21001–£24000 □2 £24001–£26000 □3 £26001–£30000 □4

**D** Would that be:
(per week) £571–£650 □1 £651–£750 □2 £751–£950 □3 £951 or more □4
(per month) £2476–£2800 □1 £2801–£3200 □2 £3201–£4100 □3 £4101 or more □4
(per year) £30001–£33500 □1 £33501–£38500 □2 £38501–£49000 □3 £49000 or more □4

**F35** Thinking now of your household's total income, from all sources and from all household members, would you say that your household is able to make ends meet?

With great difficulty 5.1 With some difficulty 31.5 Fairly Easily 52.6 Very Easily 10.8

**F36** Do you, or does anyone else in your household, own or have regular use of a car or van?

Yes, One Car/Van 54.0 Yes, More than one Car/Van 31.8 No 14.2

**F37** In general, how good would you say your health is? Would you say it is:
Very Good 42.7 Good 39.2 Fair 16.1 Bad 1.9 Very Bad 0.2

**F38** Do you have any chronic, physical or mental health problem, illness or disability?

Yes 11.4 No 88.6

**F39** **Could you tell me:**

**1. Who is the leader of Fianna Fail?**

| | | | | | | | |
|---|---|---|---|---|---|---|---|
| Charlie McCreevy | 0.7 | Brian Cowen | 0.8 | Charlie Haughey | 0.4 | Bertie Ahern | 88.9 | Don't know | 9.3 |

**2. The Green Party recently elected a leader for the first time. Could you tell me who that is?**

| | | | | | | | |
|---|---|---|---|---|---|---|---|
| Patricia McKenna | 3.4 | John Gormley | 9.1 | Trevor Sargent | 36.2 | Roger Garland | 1.5 | Don't know | 49.9 |

**3. Who is the leader of Fine Gael?**

| | | | | | | | |
|---|---|---|---|---|---|---|---|
| Jim Mitchell | 1.1 | John Bruton | 7.9 | Michael Noonan | 72.1 | Alan Dukes | 0.3 | Don't know | 18.6 |

**4. Who is the Ceann Comhairle in the Dail (Speaker of the Dail)?** [Int. Tick (✓) one box only]

| | | | | | | | |
|---|---|---|---|---|---|---|---|
| Sean Tracey | 18.4 | Jim Mitchell | 4.1 | Sean Doherty | 4.0 | Seamus Pattisson | 16.1 | Don't know | 57.3 |

**5. Who is Ireland's European Commissioner?**

| | | | | | | | |
|---|---|---|---|---|---|---|---|
| David Byrne | 35.1 | Maire Geoghan Quinn | 5.2 | Barry Desmond | 1.5 | Padraig Flynn | 10.9 | Don't know | 47.3 |

**F40** I would like you to think now about who lives in your household. Could you please tell their (a) gender; (b) age last birthday; and finally (d) their relationship to each other. [Int. Show Card E on yellow cards.]

| No | (A) Name/Initial | (B) Sex | | (C) Age last birthday | (D) Relationship of each member to each other member. READ ACROSS THE ROWS Relationships listed on yellow card | | | | | | | | | |
|----|------------------|---------|---------|------------------|----|----|----|----|----|----|----|----|----|----|
| | | Male | Female | YEARS | No | 1 | 2 | 3 | 4 | 5 | 6 | 7 | 8 | 9 |
| 1 | Head of Household | ☐1 | ☐2 | | 1 | | | | | | | | | |
| 2 | | ☐1 | ☐2 | | 2 | | | | | | | | | |
| 3 | | ☐1 | ☐2 | | 3 | | | | | | | | | |
| 4 | | ☐1 | ☐2 | | 4 | | | | | | | | | |
| 5 | | ☐1 | ☐2 | | 5 | | | | | | | | | |
| 6 | | ☐1 | ☐2 | | 6 | | | | | | | | | |
| 7 | | ☐1 | ☐2 | | 7 | | | | | | | | | |
| 8 | | ☐1 | ☐2 | | 8 | | | | | | | | | |
| 9 | | ☐1 | ☐2 | | 9 | | | | | | | | | |

**F41** Int: Please record the person number of the respondent (1 to 9 from F40 above) _____

**F42**  **Are you the head of your household?**     Yes  48.3 → go to F44     No  51.1

**F43**  **What is/was occupation of the head of the household? Please describe as fully as possible. If farmer please record the number of acres farmed. If appropriate, please record the rank or grade, e.g. Civil Service, Gardai, Defence Forces etc**

_____

_____

**F44**  **Size of location in which household is situated:**

| | | | |
|---|---|---|---|
| Open Country | 31.1 | Waterford City | 0.5 |
| Village (200–1,499) | 7.5 | Galway City | 1.6 |
| Town (1,500–2,999) | 3.9 | Limerick City | 2.3 |
| Town (3,000–4,999) | 4.4 | Cork City | 3.9 |
| Town (5,000–9,999) | 6.6 | Dublin City (incl. Dun Laoghaire) | 19.9 |
| Town (10,000 or more) | 12.1 | Dublin County (outside Dublin city) | 6.1 |

**Interviewer Record Time (24 hour clock)**

| | | | |
|---|---|---|---|
|  |  |  |  |

**F45**